THE
QUOTABLE
BOB DOLE

THE
QUOTABLE
BOB DOLE

WITTY, WISE AND OTHERWISE

JON MARGOLIS

AVON BOOKS  NEW YORK

THE QUOTABLE BOB DOLE is an original publication of Avon Books. This work has never before appeared in book form.

AVON BOOKS
A division of
The Hearst Corporation
1350 Avenue of the Americas
New York, New York 10019

Copyright © 1996 by Jon Margolis
Cover photos by David Allen c/o LGI Photo Agency; Mark Reinstein c/o FPG International; The Bettmann Archives
Published by arrangement with the author
Library of Congress Cataloging Card Number: 95-42230
ISBN: 0-380-78585-4

Library of Congress Cataloging in Publication Data:
Margolis, Jon.
  The quotable Bob Dole : witty, wise and otherwise / Jon Margolis.
     p.   cm.
1. Dole, Robert J., 1923– —Quotations. 2. United States—Politics and government—1981–1989—Quotations, maxims, etc. 3. United States—Politics and government—1989–1993—Quotations, maxims, etc. 4. United States—Politics and government—1993– —Quotations, maxims, etc. I. Dole, Robert J., 1923–. II. Title.
E840.8.D64A25 1996   95-42230
973.929'092—dc20   CIP

First Avon Books Trade Printing: April 1996

AVON TRADEMARK REG. U.S. PAT. OFF. AND IN OTHER COUNTRIES, MARCA REGISTRADA, HECHO EN U.S.A.

Printed in the U.S.A.

OPM   10   9   8   7   6   5   4   3   2

Contents

Introduction

In politics, as in comedy, timing is everything, and Bob Dole's timing seemed a bit off in 1972. A year earlier he had become chairman of the Republican National Committee, which at the time had looked like a promising spot for an ambitious young senator.

But one June night in 1972, some guys who had friends in the White House got caught breaking into the offices of the Democratic National Committee, and all of a sudden being the official leader of the entire Republican Party became a touch awkward. Even as Nixon press secretary Ron Zeigler was dismissing the whole thing as a "third-rate burglary," Dole's political antennae were sending him warnings.

Happily for Dole, he still had his comedy timing. "It was my night off," he would say. Or "I was pulling a job in Chicago that night." Or "well, we got the burglar vote."

Then, a few months after the 1972 election, he got lucky. Richard Nixon did him a big favor. He fired him as Republican National Committee chairman. Nixon didn't do it as a favor. He did it as a puritan, which he was. Dole had gotten divorced. Nixon didn't hold with divorces. Besides, Dole really was a Republican—as opposed to a Nixon—loyalist. Nixon didn't hold with that either.

As was his wont (and because he had no choice) Dole took his firing gracefully. He flew to Camp David to get the unwanted word in the company of Attorney General Richard Kleindeinst, who was also being fired. "Did you bring your rope?" Dole asked. Then, ever the good soldier, Dole agreed to hold a joint press conference to introduce his replacement.

Dole arrived in plenty of time for the press conference. The chairman-designate did not. "Where's your successor?" asked one of the reporters. Dole, alone behind the lectern, did not miss a beat. "They're dragging him in right now," he said.

From this little tale flow four truths about Bob Dole, not to mention his wit, his wisdom, and the occasional lack thereof. The first and most obvious is that unlike so many prominent political leaders, this one really has wit. The typical politician can barely manage to read the joke his speechwriter has put at the beginning of the text (though few are as dense as the former senator from New Mexico who actually read from a podium the speechwriter's *press release,* complete with the words, "Senator Montoya said yesterday"). But Bob Dole is a genuinely funny fellow. Dole has speechwriters. But they don't come up with the repartee.

Nor is Dole's humor limited to the quick one-liner. He is a Kansan, and on the prairie the preferred joke is not the quick quip; it is the drawn-out story. Dole can do both. One of the best comedy acts in American politics is his account of the night he was "Congressman Doyle," the star of an Indiana Republican dinner.

The second truth, also not universal among politicians, is that the wit is part of a package that includes some real wisdom. Dole is a funny fellow. He is not *just* a funny fellow. "They're dragging him in" was funny. It was also astute political analysis. Dole's wit meets the dictionary's first definition—"intellect, sagacity"—as well as the fourth—"ready appreciation of humor."

Although he may be a funny guy, Dole is a very serious senator. The majority leader has no choice. Some senators can just make outrageous speeches and look good. Leaders have to get bills passed. Dole may be adept at parody, but he really understands parity, that exotic formula that has been important in establishing farm price supports.

Another truth is that Dole's wit is omnidirectional.

Some of it is directed at others and his political enemies, some is directed at himself and his political
allies. Several politicians are adept at making fun of
their foes. Apart from Dole, it is hard to think of any
recent major politician who regularly poked fun at
himself unless that politician's full name was Morris
Udall or his last name was Kennedy. Toward the
end of his political career, and after it ended, Ronald
Reagan would occasionally make sport of his age.
But somebody else wrote that stuff.

Yet another truth arises indirectly from that 1973
press conference. The successor being dragged in (actually, he was just late) was a guy named Bush—
George Herbert Walker Bush, who then and later was
not Bob Dole's favorite fellow.

As everyone knows, that was not the last time
these two men bumped into each other politically.
One of the subsequent occasions was the evening of
Tuesday, February 16, 1988, primary night in New
Hampshire.

It was not a good night for Dole. As recently as the
previous Friday, he had expected to win the primary,
knock Bush out of the race, and win the Republican
presidential nomination. Instead, he got clobbered.

Then he got surprised. As he was being inter-
viewed on NBC by Tom Brokaw, live from his hotel,
who should show up in the NBC studio in Manches-
ter but Bush, the night's big winner. Brokaw asked
Bush if he had a message for Dole, and Bush replied,

"No. Just wish him well and meet in the South."
(Verbs, you may recall, were never Bush's strong
suit.)

Then, naturally, Brokaw put the same question to
Dole, who did not miss a beat this time, either. "Stop
lying about my record," he barked into the camera,
in full view of the entire country. Wherein we learn
that a witty and wise fellow can also be petulant
and foolish. If the defeat did not cost Dole the 1988
nomination, the outburst did.

"Well, I probably shouldn't have said it," he later
acknowledged, "but, you know, I just put two years
of my life into the New Hampshire primary, and I
knew it was over and you see a couple of years of
your life go down the drain and what do you say?
Aw shucks? I mean, I don't know. I didn't swear or
anything. I didn't throw anything."

Nor was that his first display of nationally tele-
vised spleen. As Gerald Ford's running mate, Dole
had provided the most memorable line in his 1976
debate against Walter Mondale when he said, "If we
added up all the killed and wounded in Democrat
wars in this century, it would be about 1.6 million
Americans, enough to fill the city of Detroit."

Democrat wars? By itself, that remark didn't lose
the 1976 election. But it helped. And Dole knew it,
and later proved that he could still turn his wit on
himself. "I was supposed to go for the jugular," he
said, "and I did—my own."

The "Democrat wars" crack also lent credence to the view that for all his irreverence, Dole is something of a bitter fellow, one whose political views are based on his resentment against Franklin Roosevelt, who led the country into the war that cost Dole the use of his right hand and arm.

That view is extreme, but not entirely unfounded. Until World War II, Dole was not a Republican. He may not have been a loyal Democrat (he wasn't all that interested in politics) but his parents were. When he started his political career as a young attorney in Russell, Kansas, the Democrats wooed him to run on their ticket. He went with the Republicans and later explained the decision with a typically pragmatic, and self-deprecating, one-liner: "There were twice as many Republicans in Russell County. So I made an on-the-spot philosophical judgment that I'd always wanted to be a Republican." There were more Republicans in Russell County, and Dole always wanted above all else to win. But that didn't mean he wasn't (and still isn't) bitter about the war.

So it hasn't been easy for Dole to live down the reputation of being a "hatchet man," and it may be significant that it was a fellow Republican senator, William Saxbe of Ohio, who first called him that. Dole knows this is a problem. Once, when a sympathetic reporter observed to him, "I don't think you've damaged anybody's reputation," Dole shot back, "No, only mine."

All that, though, is merely debatable. What is certain is that for the next few months, if not the next several years, Bob Dole is going to be a major figure in American life. At the time of this writing, he is the early front-runner for the 1996 Republican presidential nomination. This is no guarantee that he will be the nominee. Republicans don't always nominate their early front-runner. Why, as recently as 1940, they failed to do so, choosing Wendell Wilkie over Robert Taft. Ever since, though, whoever started out in front ended up that way. This renders it likely that most of us will be seeing a good deal of Dole, at least until November of 1996.

After which he would either be president of the entire United States, or merely still the Republican leader of the Senate. Considering the present political dynamic, the Republican leader is likely to continue running the joint.

So Dole's wit, his wisdom, and his foolishness are matters of some interest. In some cases, to be sure, whether he is being wise or otherwise is in the political eye of the beholder. In general, conservatives are more likely than liberals to be delighted by the Dole wit. But there are enough exceptions to this rule to please those of any ideology. Or none.

And as everyone who follows politics knows, there is far more to it and to its pursuit than mere issues.

The voters, themselves nonideological, tend to care more about the man (so far they have always been men) than his policy positions. What a politician says is often less important than the way he says it.

Dole says it quite well indeed. He has timing. He also has poise, an expressive face that he can turn from dour to pixieish, a deep baritone voice, and eyes that twinkle when he's being funny, but glower when he's angry.

Like most politicians who have been around for a while, Dole defies easy categorization. In praise of Dole, one of his former Republican colleagues, John Danforth of Missouri, once proclaimed, "He's not a bomb thrower; he's a legislator."

In fact, he has, in his long career, been both. When he first came to Congress in the 1960s, an angry and hard-line conservative, even many of his fellow Republicans found him hard to take. Years later, even many of the Democratic senators who fought him on most issues found him engaging and honorable. "Bob Dole has grown" was the 1982 judgment of no less a liberal than George McGovern. And Daniel Patrick Moynihan, the Democratic senator from New York, called him "a man of conscience, a certain hard-bitten conscience."

Even the one man who might be said to have the most reason to nurture an anti-Dole grudge later became an admirer. That was Dr. Bill Roy, the physician who came perilously close to defeating Dole in

1974, when the Watergate scandal made reelection tough for all Republicans.

This was Dole's closest race, and one of only two in which there were any allegations that he engaged in what might be called dirty politics. Roy was a pro-choice Roman Catholic, and as a physician he had performed a few therapeutic abortions. When Dole spoke at Catholic schools, he would conclude by telling the kids, "When you go home, ask your mother if she knows how many abortions Dr. Roy has performed."

In their one debate, Dole angrily asked Roy, "Why do you do abortions? And why do you favor abortion on demand?" On the Sunday before the elections, worshipers emerging from Catholic churches found on their windshields leaflets featuring photos of fetuses stuffed into garbage cans. Dole always insisted he was not involved in the leafletting.

Dr. Roy never accepted that. Still, by 1987, he said he thought Dole was doing a "good job."

By then, newspapers and magazines were full of articles about the "new" Bob Dole—calmer and more relaxed as a person, gentler and more moderate as a politician. He supported food stamps, consumer protection, civil rights. Was he becoming a centrist?

Not really. First of all, those stories were always a bit simplistic. Even in his arch-conservative days, Dole voted with moderates and liberals on some issues, especially civil rights. He never saw that as liberalism. "I believe in freedom and opportunity for people, and that's a conservative approach," he said.

Besides, by the mid-1990s, the hard-line conservative Dole had reappeared, attacking some of the very positions the "new" Dole had taken just a few years earlier. He was still charming, graceful, less contentious in person. But on most of the issues, he was moving back to the right.

This is not terribly unusual in politics. People change their minds. Ronald Reagan once favored legal abortions and Bill Clinton once didn't. Robert Kennedy began his public life as an admirer (and employee) of Joseph McCarthy and ended it as a champion of the underdog and the rebellious. Franklin Roosevelt pledged while campaigning in 1932 that he would balance the budget.

Besides, even as he moved rightward, Dole took care to distinguish himself from the right wing ideologues who, he scoffed, "all want to get up and shout about how awful the government is."

Still, it was no liberal Democrat who said, "Bob waits to see which way the wind is blowing. There's always a question: Does he have a vision? You won't see him creating an agenda." It was Nancy Landon Kassebaum, the other Republican senator from Kansas.

The record provides some justification for Senator Kassebaum's questions. Dole has been a superb legislative technician. He has not been a legislative innovator. There are plenty of bills that passed because of Dole. There is no major piece of legislation known as "The Dole Bill."

Dole knows he's a bit of a mystery. "I may not be totally predictable," he once said. "I'm not certain that's all bad."

So who is the real Robert J. Dole? Well, let him tell you. Come along for a brief ride through the rhetoric, the questions, the answers, the anecdotes and the one-liners of Bob Dole. The purpose of this exercise is neither to praise nor to condemn, neither to inspire support for Dole nor to arouse opposition to him. It is simply to explain who he is as both a person and a politician, and perhaps to reveal, largely through his own words, what kind of president he would be.

It's a window on his mind and his soul, a mind and soul worth knowing about these days. Who is this fellow? What does he believe? Where does he come from, and where would he take the country? Knowing this could be important.

And finding out can be fun. Not every minute of it, of course. Politics and government are serious business. Substantive discussion of governmental policy tends to be a dry affair, and most political rhetoric is stilted and trite. Dole has participated in his share of both. He can deliver grandiose policy statements in stentorian tones. He can engage in such clichéd political jargon as, "He not only brings home the bacon, he brings home the whole hog."

You have to figure a speechwriter wrote that one, but not the response Dole gave the night after he turned in a somnolent performance during a Republican presidential debate late in 1987. The next day he was in Hollywood, and a reporter asked him how the debate went. "Forever," Dole said.

Or the response to a reporter who asked him his impression after his next trip to Camp David, sixteen years later, this time because his wife was in the cabinet, George Bush's cabinet. "Senator," said the reporter, "how was Camp David? Was it beautiful?"

Without breaking stride, Dole shot back, "It would have been."

And regardless of his politics, or yours, it is hard not to honor the man who saw former presidents Carter, Ford, and Nixon enter the White House, gazed waspishly on them, and delivered this classic description: "See no evil. Hear no evil. And evil."

CHAPTER ONE

Dole on Dole

Bob Dole is a vain man.

Bob Dole is an ambitious man.

But he is not a stupid man. He knows he is imperfect and limited. Because he is vain and ambitious, he neither likes nor accepts those limits and imperfections. But because he's not stupid, he recognizes them. And jokes about them carefully, because he knows that while being funny is good politics, being a wise guy is not.

"I've had people tell me if they want a comedian they'll vote for Jack Benny. Then, too, people tell me if you let the critics get to you, you won't be Bob Dole. I only use humor when it's appropriate. I never tell dirty stories, and I think I have a good sense of self-deprecating humor. Okay, sometimes I use the needle. I once said I got a standing ovation from John

Tower[1] and I didn't know the difference. But he's a friend. It just seems to me that you can take the issues seriously, but you shouldn't take yourself too seriously."

Unlike many politicians, Dole doesn't pretend *not* to be ambitious: "I'm very competitive."

On December 16, 1986, when he announced which senators would serve on the joint committee to investigate the Iron-Contra mess, a reporter asked Dole if the scandal had not rendered worthless the 1988 Republican nomination.

Dole looked her square in the eye: "I'll take it."

Most politicians try to deny that they ever do poorly in a debate or a speech. Dole isn't exactly *happy* to admit to a bad performance. But he can face reality. The night after one especially dreary candidate debate, he told an audience, "I don't know how many people watched the debate last night. I was there. I was heavily sedated. It was my night to be nice to everybody."

In 1980, Dole came in dead last in the New Hampshire Republican primary, a result he did not try to

---

[1] The late, short senator from Texas.

deny when he went back to the state to try again for 1988. He'd typically start his speeches by saying, "You may not know this, but I ran for president."

He'd wait a moment for the nervous laughter to start, before adding, "Well, losing's tough. But you get over it."

Now the laughter would be less nervous, and Dole would let it die down before continuing: "The night after New Hampshire I went home and slept like a baby. Every two hours I woke up and cried."

The most memorable event of that New Hampshire primary campaign in 1980 was a candidate debate in Nashua, the one scheduled as a *mano-a-mano* contest between George Bush and Ronald Reagan, the one for which Bush refused to change the rules to allow the participation of the other candidates (who had shown up anyway), the one in which Reagan proclaimed, "I paid for this microphone" (a line he stole from an old Spencer Tracy movie), and made Bush seem like a petulant snob.

Well, before those fireworks, when the other four contenders were told they'd have to leave the splendid premises (a high school gym—what else?), candidates Phil Crane and Howard Baker wondered if it would be too humiliating simply to walk out.

Dole had another perspective: "Let's go. I've been thrown out of better places than this."

As he passed behind Bush's chair, though, Dole leaned over for another quiet parting word, one he did not intend to be funny: "There'll be another day, George."

Dole's reputation for being grumpy, if not downright mean, had not entirely faded by the time he announced his candidacy for 1996. As ever, one of the new candidate's first trips was to New Hampshire, where Dole proclaimed his new incarnation as follows: "You're seeing the new, relaxed Bob Dole campaigning in New Hampshire. The voice of reason. The warm, cuddly, fuzzy Bob Dole that you've always known."

When he said that, Dole may have been warm and cuddly. He was definitely seventy-one years old, with two birthdays to go before the presidential election. No one that old has ever been elected president unless he was Ronald Reagan and unless he was already president at the time. Despite his war injuries, Dole has been healthy, although he did have a "slow-growing" cancer on his prostate, which was removed during surgery in 1991. He managed even to get in a wisecrack about that: "I didn't think it would happen to me. I thought it happened only to Democrats."

As to running against a younger incumbent in 1996, Dole told the National Governors Association, "My cholesterol is lower than Clinton's, my weight's lower than Clinton's, and my blood pressure is lower. I'm not going to make health an issue in 1996." (Clinton, addressing the same group later in the day, replied, "I do want you to know that my standing heart rate, pulse rate, is much lower than Senator Dole's. But that really is not his fault. I don't have to deal with Phil Gramm every day.")

Dole only has one kidney, thanks to the infections caused by his war wound, but he has clearly managed to live a vigorous life that way.

His only other physical problem is that he's color blind.

Not everyone knows that. During the 1976 campaign, the GOP high command in Washington peppered the Dole campaign plane with color-coded briefing books. In the master briefing book, there were references such as "See green book" or "See red book." For weeks, Dole said nothing. Finally, he could take it no longer, and exclaimed, "Doesn't anyone on this plane know I'm color blind?"

Campaign aides then stuck labels on the books: THIS IS THE GREEN BOOK. THIS IS THE RED BOOK.

Fortunately, he's hardly the oldest senator, which at least provides the opportunity for a quip. "Every time I look at Strom Thurmond, I feel like a child." Thurmond is ninety-two years old.

And before anyone even asks him about his vim and vigor, Dole will say, "Follow me. Just follow me around for a few days. I've got a lot of stamina. I'm ready to go."

As Bob Dole once said, "Who is this person who wants to be president? What makes him tick? What's he like when he's not standing up in front of an audience?"

He's a tough taskmaster who often tells his aides, "I want it done, I want it right, I want it now, and I want no more excuses."

He's such a tough taskmaster that he's said to many a speechwriter, "Is this the best you can do?" (One, asked the question after four drafts of the same speech, finally shouted back, "Yes," whereupon Dole said, "Okay. I'll read it now.")

He's proud of where he came from, and of how far he's come from there. "I know a little about real people and real problems. I know precisely where I'm from. I think I have been tested in my lifetime."

He's happy with himself. "I think I'm a good person. I'm not perfect, but I'm workin' on it."

He's very, very proud. He always wanted to be president, but he also worried about the risk losing would impose to his reputation and image. "I don't want to be a eunuch in this town."

He is, for a public man, often quite reticent to talk

about himself. "During the '88 campaign, people kept saying, 'You gotta talk about yourself. 'Cause everybody out there in the audience has had a tough time.' Well, that's hard for me to do. I don't know if it's generational. You want to get up and talk about yourself, how tough it was, how you had all these problems in the hospital. You can be too self-serving in this business."

He can be emotional. Right after the Republican convention in 1976, the Ford-Dole ticket headed for Dole's hometown, Russell, Kansas, and Dole made his first speech as a national candidate from a stage set up on the courthouse lawn, packed tight with his Kansas neighbors, some of them the same ones who had put nickels and dimes into a cigar box to help finance the operation he needed to recover from his war wounds. "If I have had any success, it is because of the people here. I can recall the time when I needed help, and the people of Russell helped."

Then he stopped. He hadn't *meant* to stop. But he could not go on. He was sobbing for a full minute, until Jerry Ford got up and started to applaud. Then all the thousands packed onto the courthouse lawn started to applaud, until Dole could continue: "That was a long time ago. And I thank you for it."

He's a fierce partisan, but he's also been in Washington long enough to understand the political game. "Republicans figure out what is best for them, and

Democrats figure out what is best for them, and nobody figures out what is best, period."

He is part of the governing establishment, and often enough he acts the part. When Bill Clinton was elected, Dole said, "My view is that they deserve some time to get things under way." That was just a couple of days after he'd blasted Clinton's "awful" policies.

As part of the governing establishment, Dole knows that there are times when Republicans and Democrats have common interests. After the April 1995 bombing in Oklahoma City, he was philosophical, not partisan. "My mom has an expression—'Out of everything bad, something good should come, or we paid a dear price for nothing.' If there's any time the American people expect us to act in a bipartisan way, this is the time. This is the time."

Once, Dole went to Texas to campaign for the Republican opponent of Senator Lloyd Bentsen, a longtime Dole colleague. "They had me set up to call him a raging liberal. But I told them that's not the case."

He's a political pro. Which means he knows how to win, and how to lose. It means he knows when he's going to lose.

A few days after George Bush beat him in New Hampshire in 1988, Dole met with a few aides in a

South Dakota hotel room, and put this question to them: "What's the strategy?"

When no one answered him, he answered himself: "We don't have one." But like any good politician, he keeps going.

"I never give up. I figure if they're not for me they must be undecided and maybe they'll come our way."

A few days after losing the vice presidency in 1976, a friend asked Dole if he'd ever run for national office again. "Not for four years" was the reply.

Sometimes, losing brings out his bitterness. When enough Republicans voted for President Clinton's 1994 crime bill to enact it into law, Dole was not pleased. "I assume that the headlines will read, 'Republicans hand Clinton a victory.'"

But he blamed no one but himself. "I regret that I failed as a leader to keep our people together."

Dole knows that in today's anti-Washington, anti-incumbent climate, being part of the governing establishment has its drawbacks. He knows what some opponents will say: "It's Bob Dole, the insider, you know—the insider, the insider, the insider. Or the partisan, the partisan, the partisan. Or the deal maker, the deal maker, the deal maker. They think: 'Bob Dole. He's out there just cutting up everybody.' "

And he can be contemplative about the vagaries of politics. "I've watched the backslappers. I've seen people who've pushed the envelope too far. They're trying to curry favor with this group or that group. I think—'I don't want to be like this person.' I listen to all these politicians. They were all born in a log cabin. Give me a break."

And, at least most of the time, he manages to avoid the occupational hazard of politics—whining. "I've always had the attitude that you can't keep fighting last year's battles. I mean, you've got to move on, and you have disappointment and you have a loss, then you have victory, whatever. But I think overall, I've been pretty fortunate in my lifetime."

CHAPTER TWO

Humble Beginnings

Bob Dole was born on July 22, 1923, in Russell, Kansas.

In a house. Hospitals were for richer folks than Doran Dole and his wife, Bina. The house, Dole regrets, is no longer there. "They tore it down. I should have bought it. They offered it to me for $2,500. It had one bedroom, a living room, and one little kitchen."

He does own the house where he grew up, a one-story brick home on the corner of Eleventh and Maple. "Four of us kids and my parents lived in the basement apartment for years so we could get the rent money from renting out the ground floor. My father ran a creamery and a grain elevator. My mother sold sewing machines and gave sewing lessons. I'm the only one who had a college education. My sister Norma Jean went one year."

The Doles were not wealthy, to say the least. Before Bob was born, right after Doran came back from *his* war, he had used his army pay to rent a little place on Main Street which he operated as a cafe called the White Front. But not enough folks in and around Russell had the price of a meal in those days, and the cafe flopped. After that, Doran Dole sometimes managed a grain elevator, sometimes delivered butter and eggs. Bina Dole worked, too. She sold sewing machines.

Everybody in town liked Doran. He was hardworking and patient. He could also be funny, in that deadpan, midwestern manner his son would inherit. When farmers would bring their grain to the elevator, Doran would urge them to visit awhile and have a cup of his extra-strong coffee. "Sit down," he would say. "Doesn't matter if you work. The government will keep you."

Doran made more jokes than money. But there was nothing new about this. As Dole remembered, nobody in the family had ever had any money. "My grandfather, Joseph Talbott, lost all his land in the Depression. My other grandfather, Robert Grand Dole, was a tenant farmer. He never had a lot of money. As county attorney, I used to have to sign papers for his welfare payment every month. Which is a hard thing to do. So we don't come from any money in our family. I'm a little sensitized to people who work hard all their lives and don't quite make it."

One way or another, Robert Joseph Dole was going to make it. And the only way he knew how was by working. Even as a kid, Dole worked—milking cows, digging weeds, delivering groceries. By the time he was in high school, he was working afternoons and Saturdays at Dawson's Drugstore.

It was the ideal place for a young man to refine his comic talents. Customers expect the soda jerk to be quick with a quip, and Dawson's was noted as the repository of town gossip and of genial insults. When customers would ask Dole the latest gossip, one of the Dawson brothers would sometimes teasingly wonder why anybody would ask the soda jerk. Dole learned to shoot back. "Well, somebody had to have the intelligence to mix a milkshake around here."

Then and now, Russell was a town of some 5,500 people, out in the west Kansas prairie, surrounded by nothing but wheat fields, occupied only by men and women who had neither money nor power. Whatever else Dole has, he has humble beginnings, and he's kind of proud of it. "The point is, where did we start in this life. I know where I started. And know how I got where I am. Just because I've been somewhat successful, it's been sort of the American dream. Nobody gave it to me. I didn't have rich and powerful parents. I made it the hard way. I worked at it."

Hard work wasn't the only thing Dole had going for him. He was tall, handsome, and smart. He was a good athlete, too. Or maybe it's more accurate to say he *made* himself into a good athlete. He lifted weights. He ran everywhere, and got fast enough to make the track team, running the half-mile. He played football, too, and he was the star of the high school basketball team, no small matter in Kansas. He was going to ride that ability all the way to the state university in Lawrence. He was going to be a doctor.

It looked like it was working. Basketball helped him get into the university. It wasn't the kind of full-ride athletic scholarship kids get today. But it was an invitation to enter the University of Kansas and try out for the team. He could wait on tables for spending money. So he went off to college in September 1941, just about two months before the attack on Pearl Harbor.

CHAPTER THREE

Dole at War

Dole was not gung-ho to go to war.

Western Kansas was a long way from the oceans, and there was always a bit of an isolationist streak there. Besides, he was having too much fun at the University of Kansas. He was in a fraternity. He was playing sports. He was going out with pretty girls. More than a year after Pearl Harbor, he was still at school.

But he knew he'd be drafted, so he signed up for the Army Enlisted Reserve Corps, which at least let him finish the term. He didn't head off to basic training until mid-1943. By the spring of 1944, he had applied for officer training, and when he finished officer candidate school at Fort Benning, Georgia, D-Day had come and gone. Maybe he wouldn't get to fight.

Then the army did one of those things which only armies do. "I was not a skier. I am not a mountain climber. I came from the plains of Kansas and wound up in the mountain division."

He was commander of the Second Platoon of the Third Battalion of the Eighty-fifth Mountain Regiment, to be precise, slogging through Italy's Po Valley in the early months of 1945. He was a rookie in command of seasoned troops who had lost half their officers in a bloody assault on a hill called Mount Belvedere.

The new lieutenant was plain-spoken: "I'm Lieutenant Dole. I'm going to be leading the platoon. Dole, like the pineapple juice."

The new lieutenant was also smart. A veteran sergeant was effectively running the platoon, and Dole told him, "All right, soldier, there won't be any changes. We'll run it like you've been running it, until we get the knack of it."

He didn't get too much time. Less than six weeks later, on April 14, the day after Franklin Roosevelt died, Dole's company moved out on the left flank of a "breakout" designed to take a hill. Dole's platoon was to go down a slope and across a valley, then over a stone fence and up the hill. As he remembered it later, "It kicked off, as I recall, not real early in the morning, about 9:45, from somewhere off over in those mountains somewhere, coming down a narrow road, then up through some mountain pass."

They were fine until they crossed the wall and started uphill. Then some of the men were pinned down by a German machine-gun nest. There was no choice but to send the lead squad against the machine-gunners. The top sergeant thought he'd lead the assault, but Dole said, "Sergeant, I'll take them."

He got about sixty yards before the German machine-gunners spotted him and his troops. He threw a grenade that fell short, then dived into a shell-hole for cover. For a moment, he was safe there. But not all of his men could find cover. "My radio guy's name was Symms and he had been hit. I was trying to get him back into this little ravine, and once I was backed in there, I must have raised up.

"I remember getting a sharp sting in my right, the back of my right shoulder. I knew something happened and then I couldn't move, and somebody turned me over and my arms were above my head and I couldn't move my arms and, you know, then I knew something was wrong."

His men dragged him into a gully where they were sheltered. They called for medics, but two of them got killed trying to get there.

"Pretty soon somebody came by and gave me, I think a shot of morphine, and I was told later they didn't have anything to mark it with, so they just marked it with my blood."

That somebody was not a medic. But Sergeant Stan Kuschik of Dole's platoon had morphine with him.

This was probably against the rules. It was certainly smart, and it was one of several accidents that saved Dole's life.

Not being a medic, Kuschik didn't have one of those crayons to mark a tan M on the forehead, to warn other medics not to administer any more morphine. That's why he used Dole's blood.

Then he broke another rule, the one that said no able-bodied men were to be left behind with the wounded. He ordered a soldier to stay with Dole.

Cold and semiconscious, Dole lay there, able to ask but one question: "How bad is it?" The soldier told him he'd be fine. He didn't believe it. "And I must say my whole life raced in front of me. I saw my dog. I saw my parents. I saw my family, I saw my hometown. Then I didn't see anything for a long, long time."

Was he brave?

"I don't know if I was ever brave. You know, there are some people who do things like fall on a grenade or stand in front of something to protect somebody. I didn't have that kind of experience, and that's bravery to me."

Nine hours later he got to the hospital. He ended up being in a lot of hospitals.

"I happened to be in the wrong place at the wrong time. As a result of that I got to spend the next thirty-nine months in and out of hospitals."

That's how he put it later, when he could be funny

about it. At the time, he was often depressed. "I went through a period of almost complete dependence. Even in the bathrooms, they had to come in and help you. You go through this period, and you almost get stubborn the other way—'I don't want anybody to help me. I can get it myself. Don't touch me.'"

But he didn't give up. In fact, for quite a while he deluded himself into thinking he could make a complete recovery, returning not just to college but to sports. He kept squeezing rubber balls to try to regain strength in his useless right hand. He thought he'd play basketball again.

Instead, he barely lived. More than once, he almost didn't. He got pneumonia twice, and the second time he only survived because streptomycin had just been discovered. When doctors gave it to Dole, it was still an experimental drug. It saved his life.

Back home in Russell, he dragged himself down to Dawson's Drugstore one day. The big, strapping, local hero who'd gone to war weighed 122 pounds, and he needed help to sit on one of the counter stools. A not very tactful customer who might have thought he was being nice mentioned something about how Dole probably wished the Germans had killed him on the spot. Dole turned to him. "If I thought like that, I'd have been dead a long time ago."

If he was determined, he was still depressed, as he later acknowledged: "You sort of get bitter at everybody. Then you decide that you'll live with it, make the most of it, and make it work for you."

Later, a doctor named Hampar Kelikian made Dole as whole as anyone could. In three operations, Dr. Kelikian repositioned Dole's right arm so that it hung at his side and gave him some movement in his right hand and arm. He also convinced Dole that there would be no miracle, that his right arm would never be capable of full rotation, the right hand never able to do much more than hold something lightly.

It took a while, but the message sunk in, and the kid who was going to be a doctor, the athlete who was going to return to the basketball court, accepted the reality of his situation. "The only thing I've got left is my head, so I'd better use it."

As to sports: "Politics was a natural substitute for athletics ... much of my life since April 1945 has been an exercise in compensation. Maybe I couldn't use my hand, I told myself, but I could develop my mind."

And his character: "Physical limitations teach perseverance and humility."

Humility is not a word usually associated with Dole. But perseverance is. All the years of recovery, the adjustment to things like getting through law school without being able to take notes, or not being able to button your own shirt or knot your own tie, which was still a problem for him as recently as the mid-1980s. "Some days I just can't do it. I can't get a tux on. That's why I turn down a lot of black-tie dinners."

But if Dole occasionally despaired, he never quit. He once said, "Whatever else I am, I'm a survivor."

Not, to be sure, an unscathed survivor. There are still days he doesn't like to look into a mirror. "I guess it goes back to the first day I got out of bed in Topeka, Kansas, in 1945. I'd been very sick. I'd gone down to about 120 pounds from 194, and I looked in the mirror and I just—I mean I didn't know who this person was."

And he surely has not forgotten April 14, 1945: "We had 553 men killed or wounded in our division. That's a pretty good number. That's a very tough day's work.

"We were all scared to death. I mean, people who tell you they weren't scared, in my view, weren't there. And some of us were just lucky enough to be at the wrong place at the wrong time. But the ones that, you know, that really deserve our respect are the ones that never made it, died there."

CHAPTER FOUR

The Young Politician

Aside from talking, somewhat reluctantly, about recovering from his wounds, Dole has not said much about either his private life or his political career in the years right after World War II.

There isn't that much to say. In 1948, while he was recuperating at the Percy Jones Army Medical Center in Michigan, he met a therapist named Phyllis Holden. Contrary to some later Kansas folklore, she never was *his* therapist. But she did become his wife and the mother of his one child, Robin.

Nor is there much to say about Dole's early political career. By his own accounting he "sorta fell into politics." At the age of twenty-six, he ran for the legislature while at Washburn University Law School in Topeka. It met for only three months during his single two-year term.

Then he decided to run for county attorney. It was a good job for a young lawyer. The pay was only $248 a month (the courthouse janitor earned more), but you could make good contacts. And while campaigning, you could get some good stories, such as the one about the farmer who greeted Dole at the door and told him he'd known his grandfather. "Good," said Dole, whereupon the following dialogue ensued.

"Used to butcher for me."

"Yeah, he was a pretty good butcher."

"No he wasn't. Gave me bad sausage. Never liked him."

As all young politicians do, Dole used his position to make contacts in case he wanted to run for higher office. As he put it, "Most politicians sort of do an internship—go through Kiwanis and Red Cross, become well known in the community, Boy Scouts, Chamber of Commerce."

In 1960, Dole ran for Congress. In what was then a safe Republican district, the real contest was in the primary, where his leading opponent was Keith Sebelius, a popular attorney from nearby Norton, who was also a former official of the American Legion.

Dole had two problems. First of all, there was a third candidate, a state senator named Phil Doyle.

"Doyle" sounds a lot like "Dole." So Dole used the pineapple connection to make sure voters could tell the difference.

His other problem was that Sebelius was using the American Legion membership list for his campaign mailings. With some justification, Dole thought this was unfair.

But then another mailing made its way through the district. These letters, many bearing Washington state postmarks, suggested that Sebelius was a drunk. Pretty soon, there was a lot of whispering around western Kansas that Keith Sebelius drank too much. Aside from the letters and the whispering, there was no evidence whatsoever that Sebelius had a drinking problem.

Was Dole behind this? "I don't know where it came from," he has said.

No one ever proved that Dole was behind the mailings. But when Keith Sebelius died in 1982, his family quite pointedly did *not* invite Bob Dole back to their house after the funeral.

Bob Dole and John Kennedy both took their new offices in 1961. Dole opposed Kennedy's politics, but accepted the invitation to the White House Christmas party. He danced with his wife, Phyllis, and also with the wives of his Kansas colleagues, including Rose Mary McVey, wife of Representative Walter McVey from Independence. The marine band played "Mr. Wonderful," and Rose Mary observed that this was a perfect evening. Dole replied, "Live it up while you can, Rose Mary. We're parked in a ten-minute zone."

Even as a first-termer, Dole made a bit of a splash. He took the lead in calling for congressional investigation into the affairs of Billie Sol Estes, who had made himself rich by some complex manipulation of government farm storage facilities. In May of 1962, Dole claimed that, "Members of both parties feel that the investigation has moved much too slowly, particularly as it relates to the Department of Agriculture."

The scandal turned out to be both minor and bipartisan; Estes had begun his manipulations during the Eisenhower years. But Dole got marked as a bold fellow, one who didn't mind speaking out, even at the risk of seeming a bit foolish.

In 1965, for instance, when Congress passed the Highway Beautification Act so strongly backed by Lady Bird Johnson, Dole didn't just oppose it, he proposed an amendment which would have replaced the words "The Secretary of Commerce" wherever they appeared in the bill, with the words "Lady Bird."

Not "The First Lady," but "Lady Bird."

It lost on a voice vote.

CHAPTER FIVE

Dole the Kansan

Some politicians forget where they come from.
Dole does not.

He's a Kansan.

Moreover, he's a west Kansan, from Russell, one of those decaying towns on the Great Plains, the kind that have been losing population steadily for decades, the kind where making a living has always been tough. He spends far more time in Washington than in Russell these days, but he still considers Kansas his home, and says so. "I'm not the first Kansan to say there's no place like home. But for me the words have special meaning. Whenever I have traveled in this life, I have never forgotten where I came from, or where I go home to."

Announcing his 1996 candidacy from the state capital in Topeka, Dole pointed out the advantages of that capital over the one where he works: "You can see many things from atop the hill in Washington where I work, but you can see America from here. Common sense and uncommon sensitivity, that's the Kansas way. It's what made Dwight Eisenhower a great general and a great president, and it's what prompted Alf Landon, with his unique wisdom to say, 'There are some intelligent people in Washington, but there are a lot more of 'em in Kansas.' "

These days, though, announcement speeches are broadcast live nationwide, so there's a limit as to how parochial a candidate can be, which Dole acknowledged in the very next sentence. "I hasten to add—I hasten to add, the same applies to the other forty-nine states, particularly Iowa and New Hampshire. But then Kansans never had to look to Washington, D.C., for a sense of compassion or community. As a young man in a small town, my parents taught me to put trust in God, not government, and never confuse the two."

If Dole had his way, presidential candidates would not have to be solicitous of Iowa and New Hampshire. "Some say we ought to change the system. And I said I agree. We ought to have Kansas. That ought to be the first state. But I couldn't get them to do that."

Not that Dole has never been parochial. To the contrary, he takes care of the home folks. It was he who got through the biggest spending of all farm bills in 1985 (about $30 billion a year at its most expensive) and who defended it in 1986. "It's a good bill. Farmers will see the effect."

They didn't, which only made Dole more defensive. "It wasn't us who called the grain embargo in 1980. We didn't cause the recession."

Dole also shepherded through the Congress the repeal of luxury taxes on private airplanes, not unaware that both the Beech and Cessna companies are in Kansas. No doubt, he's also aware that the officials and political action committees of those companies contribute generously to his campaigns, as well as to the Dole Foundation, which Dole established to promote economic independence for the disabled. The luxury tax, part of the 1990 bill which Dole also helped guide to passage, was for 10 percent on private planes costing more than $250,000.

So Dole takes care of Kansas. But he also knows them and is under few illusions about them. In 1982, when the farm economy was in the doldrums and politicians were wondering how farmers would vote, Dole was not one of those who assumed the rural affection for Ronald Reagan would necessarily carry the day. "Almost every farmer seems to personally like the president. [But if] it's a choice between their banker and loyalty to the president, I think they're going to go with their banker."

Still, Dole likes Kansans, and is convinced that they like him, too. "I've said to some people to pick up any book in Kansas, pick a name at random, call them up. And say, 'What do you think about Bob Dole?'

"Well, a few of them may hang up on you, but keep trying. Sooner or later somebody's going to say, 'Who?' or they're going to tell you, whether they're Republicans or Democrats, that Bob Dole works hard, and they'll tell you the truth."

CHAPTER SIX

Dole on Women and Marriage

Bob Dole has had two marriages.

The first one didn't work out very well.

In fact, one important quote from Bob Dole he'd probably prefer to be forgotten consists of his blunt message to his first wife, Phyllis, in 1972: "I want out."

In fact, he had wanted out earlier. It was politics, not love, that held the marriage together toward the end, as Dole later acknowledged. "I was always feeling so selfish about my future, and I wouldn't leave."

He meant his political future. Until 1980, Americans had never elected a divorced president, and in states like Kansas it was not at all certain that they would elect a divorced senator. The old "If he can't keep his marriage together how can he help run the country?'' attitude was still strong, and in an interview with journalist Myra MacPherson, Dole said he knew it. "You sorta think divorce must be a defect in somebody. You don't like it to happen, and then, you look at yourself as a politician. These things aren't *supposed* to happen to you. You're not *supposed* to be normal. You're not *supposed* to have problems."

In that same interview, he was candid about the damage politics can do to a marriage. "Whether you're driven by the excitement, or because you think you have the ability, suddenly we let our lives be taken over by politics. We find ourselves every weekend on an airplane when we should be with our families. I don't care how strong a marriage is, when you come on Sunday night and the children are going to bed and you don't see them again until Thursday and then only for a brief period of time before going out again, they literally grow up without you knowing who they are."

But he didn't use his career as an excuse. "I can quit any time I want to and there'll be a long line of people to take my place ... I found myself taking more speaking engagements. I would find something to do in the office. Maybe I didn't want to face home. I could convince myself I was overwhelmed with all this work."

But his second marriage, by all indications, is doing just fine.

Dole and Elizabeth Hanford met in 1972. He had just been divorced and she was a consumer affairs specialist in the Nixon White House.

The meeting was official business. She had to see the Republican national chairman to discuss the consumer plank in the Republican platform.

For a while, Bob Dole was Senate Republican leader and Elizabeth Dole was secretary of transportation. When Ronald Reagan nominated her for the job, her husband introduced her to the Senate Commerce Committee, which was considering the nomination.

The chairman, Senator Bob Packwood of Oregon, asked Dole (the senator, not the nominee) whether he had filed a conflict of interest statement. "I have no conflict, but there's a lot of interest. I've known the nominee for about ten years, and I regret that I have but one wife to give to my country's infrastructure. I think she's well qualified and I plan to vote for her."

Bob and Elizabeth were known as Washington's "power couple." She's no longer in government, but they still have a fair amount of clout. After leaving the cabinet, she became president of the American Red Cross. When she accompanied him on campaign fund-raising talks, he would say, "She's trying to find your vein, and I'm trying to find your wallet."

Late in 1995, Mrs. Dole took a leave of absence from the American Red Cross, but she later announced that she would return to the job even if she becomes First Lady. If Dole wins and she sticks to the plan, Mrs. Dole would become the first wife of a president to have a paying job outside of government.

At one point, the Doles were, at least theoretically, political competitors. Both of their names were on George Bush's vice presidential list in 1988, both went to the convention in New Orleans wondering what would happen, and in the view of some Republicans, Bush was more likely to choose her than him. In discussing their New Orleans hotel arrangements, Dole hinted that he agreed. "It's really her room. I'm just a poor senator. She wasn't even here and I walked in. I saw the room said, '1988.' Then I learned it was in her name. I think she's trying to tell me something."

His wife's fame and power does not seem to faze Dole. When she got the cabinet appointment, he recalled, "There were a lot of stories and a lot of pictures taken. I was always in the picture, but I was never identified. They said, 'The man on the left is the husband.' *People* magazine took an interest in Elizabeth, so a photographer followed us around and took about three hundred pictures. They wound up using three, and one showed us making the bed.

"Some guy out in California whose wife had read the story wrote that he was now helping make the bed. He said, 'Senator, I don't mind your wife getting the job. She's well qualified. She's doing good work. But you've got to stop doing the work around the house. You're causing problems for men all across the country.'

"I wrote back and said, 'Buster, you don't know the half of it. The only reason she was helping was because they were taking pictures.'"

Then there was the matter of President Reagan's veto of the $88 billion highway bill in 1987. Dole supported the veto, but not enthusiastically. The bill was popular, and many Republican senators thought the veto might plague them in the next election. But Elizabeth was Reagan's Secretary of Transportation, and her support of the president's position was ardent. It was an issue, acknowledged Dole, that "Elizabeth feels fairly strongly about."

And when Elizabeth feels strongly about something, he acknowledged, she could make folks take notice. "She's very effective, I'll tell you. I have a lot of women ask me, 'Why should she give up her job? Why don't you quit your job? It's fairly sensitive. Here's a woman—the only woman in the cabinet—she has her own identity, her own responsibility. And doing a good job at it."

On that issue, at least, the two Doles were on the same side. In 1993, Bob Dole was in charge of the Republican minority in the Senate and Elizabeth was running the Red Cross, which gave her a different perspective on some matters.

From that perspective, President Clinton's National Service Bill, which later became America-Corps, was a great idea. In a letter to Senator Edward Kennedy, the bill's Senate sponsor, Mrs. Dole said the plan "will enlarge the means by which individuals can make a difference in their community."

And what did her husband think of the bill?

"Willy-nilly mortgaging our future."

Dole's view of marriage and families was not always a bright one. At one point, after a constituent with five kids came to his Washington office, Dole asked, "How can that guy ever get anywhere, laden down like that? He's just a beast of burden."

But his second marriage seems to have changed his views on families, and perhaps on some political issues. At least, many observers have credited Elizabeth's influence on his calmer demeanor, and on some of the more moderate policy positions he has taken in recent years. Dole has never confirmed that analysis, but neither has he denied it. "Well, I think we all change. I always go back and take a look at what people say. They might be right. You may be upset at the time when somebody writes something or says something. But you never want to totally disregard it—might be a grain of truth in it. So I don't say I made any abrupt change. But at least it [his marriage] probably had an influence. Because rightly or wrongly, I got the reputation and I had to make certain that whatever was out there, I erased it or changed it."

Dole's policy positions on women's issues have been mixed. He's always been a firm opponent of abortion. He's also been a firm supporter of equal opportunity, once opposing the Reagan Administration when it tried to narrow the interpretation of the laws against sex discrimination. The administration, Dole contended, was engaged in "a legalistic, technical interpretation."

The then–attorney general, William French Smith, was not pleased.

CHAPTER SEVEN

Senator Dole

The name is Dole.

The title is Senator.

And to the man, the title is almost as important as the name.

Bob Dole is serious about being a senator.

No, it's more than that. He's serious about being a Senate leader. Not just being the majority leader when the Republicans are in charge, but about being one of the members of the Senate's inner circle, the Club, the people who run the place and make it go.

Which does not blind him to the flaws of the institution, or of its members.

For instance, when he was first elected majority leader, after the 1984 elections, Dole said, "If we really want the discipline, I'm willing to help provide it—and sometimes, if we really don't want the discipline."

Nor is he unaware that the Senate's rules often prevent it from acting quickly. "It doesn't take a rocket scientist to hold up the Senate two or three days."

Dole has been around long enough to know that the merits of an argument are often not enough, even when he is convinced of the merits, as he was of the 1990 tax and budget bill, which was designed to cut the deficit. "You have to give people some reason to vote for this. The real reason, deficit reduction, ought to be good enough, but they have to have something to take home and say, 'I won this.'"

He's also been around long enough to know the difference between a senator who really needs something to take home, and a senator who is playing games. "I think I know the players here pretty well, and I think I know when there's a genuine exchange, or when somebody's holding back something. There's got to be a time when you sort of let go, you know."

When all the debates and the anger and the rhetoric are over, Dole knows, "The bottom line in this place is how many votes do you have."

One of the Senate's problems Dole understands because he's part of it—most senators think they should be president, some day if not now. He once suggested that the Senate set aside a daily "presidential hour," divided into four segments.

"First, those senators who think they are president. Second, those who think they should have been president. Third, those who want to be president. And fourth, those who are willing to settle for vice president."

But in true Dole fashion, he doesn't entirely exclude himself from this particular weakness. "I've found only one senator who didn't want to be president—and when I asked him for an affidavit, he declined. I think at one time or another we all think we're smart enough, but it probably isn't going to happen."

For all his irreverence, Dole has high regard for the Senate and its traditions. When he violated one of those traditions, back in 1971, he was quick to make amends. And a joke.

"I introduced a resolution which Senator J. William Fulbright claimed he had already sponsored. 'Stealing a man's amendment is like stealing his cow,' Fulbright complained. But I reminded him that it was National Dairy Week and I would never steal a man's cow during National Dairy Week. I just milked it a little."

Dole became majority leader for a second time after the 1994 elections, when Republicans also took over the House of Representatives, whose new leaders shook up the old rules. Dole didn't. "On the Senate side, the agenda's going to be controlled by a consensus, by leadership working with committee chairmen."

Chairmen, he made clear, would continue to be chosen through seniority. When some commentators, and a few Republicans, wondered about the wisdom of having the ultraconservative and uncompromising Senator Jesse Helms of North Carolina assume the gavel of the Foreign Relations Committee, Dole cut off the speculation.

"Senator Helms will be the chairman of the Foreign Relations Committee. If you're going to start knocking down seniority, there's going to be an avalanche out there because a lot of chairmen have been talked about who might be endangered. I don't think any of them are endangered. We have a seniority system. It works."

That was good news for conservatives. But also for moderates who worried that the more conservative senators would try to displace Senator John Chafee of Rhode Island from the chairmanship of the Environment and Public Works Committee. Chafee supports more stringent environmental regulations than do many Republicans, including Dole.

Nor did Dole offer any support to those who would do away with the most controversial of the Senate's peculiar rules—the filibuster. "It doesn't just

protect the interests of a partisan minority, but also
the interests of economic and geographic minorities,
including individual states.''

Like the comedian who has been rich and poor,
and prefers being rich, Dole has led Republicans as
both the minority and the majority, and he far prefers
the latter. Senate majorities pass laws, which is what
Dole likes to do. Senate minorities make trouble. He
likes to do that, too, but less.

When he was minority leader in 1992, he worried
about losing more seats that year. With fewer members, he said, ''All you could do is frustrate the majority. You couldn't deal with them. You could
frustrate them, drag things along, irritate people,
which you'd have to do. You wouldn't have much
impact on the results. Keep a lot of people awake,
though.''

As Dole remembers it, he was as surprised as anyone when he first learned that the Republicans had
a real shot at taking over the Senate in 1980. Howard
Baker, then the Republican leader, called Dole shortly
before the election to tell him that the party's polling
showed they just might gain the majority for the first
time in twenty-five years, and that if they did, Dole
would be chairman of the Finance Committee.

''I said, 'Howard, that's great. But who's going to

tell Senator Russell Long, because he's been chairman of that committee for seventeen years.'

"And we had to have little instructions and little classes on how to conduct a meeting. We never thought we'd be chairmen of anything. So a lot of people were skeptical about me. In any event—so we had these little classes on how to conduct a meeting: how to rap the gavel, how to look straight at the witness while sleeping, and a lot of things."

Even Dole was surprised at how easy some of it was. "Ronald Reagan's first program to come to Congress was tax reduction. A lot of people said, 'You can't do it.' But he didn't know that, because he hadn't been there. So he did it anyway."

According to his own words of 1992, when he was minority leader and George Bush was president, Dole is now in his favorite position (second to the presidency, of course) because he's the majority leader and the president is of the opposing party.

"I always thought the strongest position would be the position (George) Mitchell is in—to be majority leader when the other guy is in charge downtown, and then you can pretty well bring things to a halt around here."

Which he did.

When the Senate is in session, Bob Dole is in charge.

He is the leader, and he is not pleased when any-one fails to recognize that fact, including other Republicans. Thus, when another Republican senator vowed to clutter up the health care debate by offering scads of amendments, Dole grumbled, "I haven't been advised of that. There are a lot of chiefs here."

There was but one chief. The amendments were not offered.

Even when the Republicans were in the minority, Dole did not suffer internal opposition gladly. When he was running for the 1988 presidential nomination, he didn't mind if newspaper columnists or Democrats suggested he could not be both a candidate and minority leader. When Republican Senator Lowell C. Weicker of Connecticut made the suggestion, though, Dole shot back, "I don't know what I did to him. Maybe I kept him late one night and he missed his dinner."

In a party caucus in 1991, another unhappy Republican, Malcolm Wallop of Wyoming, criticized Dole for supporting the previous year's budget agreement.

Dole said if Wallop wanted the leadership an election could be held that minute.

Wallop backed down.

In Dole's view, anybody can be a senator. Being a leader is more difficult. "You've got to make hard choices if you're going to be a leader. If you just want to be a politician you vote no against all the hard things and vote yes for all the easy things, and you go out and make speeches about how tough you are."

As majority leader the first time, he earned a reputation for being fair, but not for tolerating any challenge to his authority. During a debate in 1986 over aid to the Nicaraguan rebels, some Democrats accused Dole of dictating to the Senate. After more than an hour of partisan testiness, Dole rose, his dark eyes scowling and his voice firm and just a touch harsh. "I do not intend to be intimidated by anyone in the Senate. I did not become majority leader to lose."

In the Senate, being a leader means knowing how to play the rules.

And the angles.

Sometimes, for instance, it's good politics not to appear to be doing what you are in fact doing. So it was that when a health insurance bill which Republicans opposed came to the Senate floor in 1994, the party's chosen strategy was to delay action for as long as possible.

But they didn't want to look like obstructionists, so they never announced a filibuster. They just kept making speeches.

About which Dole said, "We're not in a filibuster. After eight or nine hours of debate, there is already the perception—and the liberal media is buying into it—that somehow the Republicans are stalling, stalling."

A year earlier, Republicans *had* mounted a filibuster—their fourth of the year—against President Clinton's national service proposal. At least Dole called in a filibuster on Friday, July 23. Six days later he said, "There hasn't been any filibuster. We've been negotiating."

As it turned out, there *was* a filibuster, but they were negotiating. And it worked. A deal was struck.

CHAPTER EIGHT

Dole the Political Analyst

Just as the lawyer who represents himself has a fool for a client, the smart politician is well advised to let the reporters and the professors analyze campaigns. Running for office is hard enough without also trying to examine your own entrails.

Alas, even the astute candidate often finds it hard to resist the temptation to punditry. Dole is no exception. Nor is he an exception to the general rule that a candidate never analyzes any race worse than the one he is in.

So it was that after his several primary losses on "Super Tuesday" in 1988, Dole proclaimed, "I am not a dropout."

Several days later, he dropped out.

And before that year's Republican National Convention in New Orleans, with Dole on most short lists for George Bush's running mate, he sounded aloof. "I don't want to go down to New Orleans and grovel around down there for the second spot."

But he went down to New Orleans anyway, waiting for the call that would name either him or his wife to the second spot. When the call came, it told them Dan Quayle had been picked.

On the other hand, Dole can exhibit an unusually detached perspective on his own political troubles, at least after the fact.

One of the things he remembered long after his defeat in the 1988 New Hampshire primary was that his pollster, Richard Wirthlin, had warned him a day or two before the voting that his support was fading.

"He was saying, 'The numbers are getting soft.' You know, pollsters never say, 'You're in trouble.' They're like economists."

At least Dole's numbers in 1988 were measurable, which could not be said about the 1980 New Hampshire primary. That was the year, Dole remembered, when "Nobody noticed I was running. Whenever I spoke, the three empty chairs got up and walked away."

And the one time he did get a national nomination—as Gerald Ford's 1976 vice presidential choice—Dole could size up his own situation realistically: "The vice presidency is a great job—it's all indoor work and no heavy lifting."

But then there was the time he summed up his own political situation most incorrectly. Early in the 1988 campaign, at a time when Dole thought he would win the nomination, he grew reflective, musing that he would win the presidency then, or never. "You know, I'm not running again. Sometimes you have to lose, and it makes you stronger. You can come back. But I'm not running again. This is my time."

Even that year, though, Dole did not fool himself often, or for long. Nor did he let his high-priced assistants fool him often or for long. After winning in Iowa, his pollster, Richard Wirthlin, explained the victory scenario. All they had to do was win New Hampshire, he said, "And then it's a roll." He looked at Dole. Dole looked back. "Wait a minute. Back up a minute. What if we don't win?"

By primary eve, Wirthlin was still telling Dole he was going to win, and Dole still wasn't being fooled. "No, I'm not. I'm going to lose by five or six."

It was worse than that.

As a general rule, working politicians are no better as political philosophers than they are as political pundits. A few politicians claim to be intellectual, but most of those claims approach the spurious. Dole, to his credit, never called himself an intellectual, and rarely aspires to the cosmic pronouncement. The closest he comes is the occasional pithy remark, such as, "The life jacket of one generation can become the straitjacket of the next."

His disinclination to engage in broad philosophical statements usually protects Dole from the errors that bedevil some politicians. Unlike Ronald Reagan, Dole rarely has to get his staff to explain away misstatements of fact.

At least not usually. In his June 13, 1995 reply to President Clinton's budget statement, Dole proclaimed that "as government has grown bigger, the plight of poor Americans has grown steadily worse."

He did not try to document that assertion.

When they are not personally involved, politicians can be astute about politics—the politics of their own party. For the most part, it is a good rule never to take seriously the thoughts of a Republican about what will happen among Democrats, and vice versa.

But on a politically important weekend in 1979, when everyone who cared watched Roger Mudd's now-famous interview with Senator Edward Kennedy on CBS, while those who did not care watched the television premiere of *Jaws* on another network, Dole summarized the situation as well as anyone.

"Seventy-five percent of the country watched *Jaws*, twenty-five percent watched Roger Mudd, and half of them couldn't tell the difference."

CHAPTER NINE

Dole the Partisan

When it comes to partisan politics, Bob Dole does not fool around.

As individuals, Democrats are acceptable to him. As a group, they are not. And sometimes he refuses to make the distinction.

He wouldn't even watch "Bonanza" at the height of its popularity because the show's stars were Democrats. In the 1960s, he summed up his opinion of Attorney General Ramsey Clark as "a left-leaning marshmallow." When Jimmy Carter first started running for president, Dole dismissed him as "Southern-fried McGovern," and "a political quick-change artist."

To Dole, Carter was just as bad as all those other Democrats, or perhaps worse. "We've had the New Deal, the Fair Deal, and now somebody wants to give us a fast deal that would surely end in an ordeal."

And though his own foreign policy attitudes tend toward caution when it comes to military involvement, Dole was unsparing toward Democratic politicians who opposed the war in Vietnam. In 1972, he described them as "A Who's Who of has-beens, would-bes, professional second-guessers, and apologists for the policies which led us into this tragic conflict in the first place."

He even said they were "parroting the propaganda of a communist enemy."

Preparing his 1980 presidential candidacy, Dole announced in August 1979 that he would aim his criticism not at President Carter but at Senator Edward Kennedy, who at the time was not a candidate. Why?

"Senator Kennedy is unique in American politics" was Dole's public reply.

But in private, he was calling Kennedy "a phony, a limousine liberal, a big spender raised on a silver spoon."

As the campaign, and Kennedy's difficulties, progressed, Dole would ridicule him as "needing a bridge over troubled waters," and "making a big splash."

This was not the first time he'd gone out of his way to attack Kennedy. In 1972, as George McGovern and Edmund Muskie vied for the Democratic presidential nomination, Dole challenged Kennedy to declare his presidential candidacy. "Kennedy is a candidate with a deliberate, thoroughly worked out game plan for winning the Democratic nomination—for whatever that nomination is worth."

That plan, Dole said, "calls for the presidential candidates to exhaust each other's resources in an inconclusive series of primary battles, so they'll turn to a man who wouldn't get his feet wet. In short, I think what we want is a little less profile and a little more courage. I ask Senator Kennedy to come out and join the struggle, to come out and try to earn what he wants."

In fact, Kennedy had no intention whatever of running for president in 1972.

For all the barbs and all their political differences, Dole and Kennedy are not entirely unfriendly. In the mid-1980s, they even did a radio show together.

Well, not exactly together. Each man taped his half of the weekly, five-minute show from his own office. Each man got $40,000 a year for his efforts. Kennedy used his money to hire more staff. Dole openly acknowledged that he kept his. "I do it for the money. I don't know why Kennedy does it."

The program was full of mock anger, precious little subtlety, and imperfect grammar. Arguing over the safety of nuclear power, Dole said to Kennedy, "Ted, for a guy who thinks 'The China Syndrome' is what you get after eating too much chop suey, I'm not about to accept you as an expert on nuclear plant technology."

In 1991, Dole was one of the speakers at a ceremony presenting Kennedy with the Claude Pepper Distinguished Service Award. He said he hoped Kennedy would serve as long as Pepper had. "Which means that he would serve until the year 2021, and he will be serving as ranking minority member of the Judiciary Committee."

Dole always knows who his adversary is. Once he was on a television program with Senator Jay Rockefeller, the West Virginia Democrat, who complained that Republicans wanted to cut the budget "to do the tax cut for the rich."

Dole pounced. "We're not using any Medicare savings for tax cuts for the rich, as I hear all my Democratic friends state—some of them rich, come to think of it."

Rockefeller did not reply.

Dole also goes right for the jugular in partisan debate on the Senate floor. When Democratic leader George Mitchell blamed Republicans and the insurance industry for scuttling President Clinton's health proposal, Dole shot back, "Senator Mitchell blames Republicans for everything except the plane that crashed into the White House."

Sometimes, though, Dole knows the value of understatement. As Congress wrapped up its business in 1993, many Republicans went into excruciating detail about how awful they thought President Clinton's budget and other policies had been. Dole was downright taciturn. The session's legislative product had been "a little too much, I think."

But Dole knows when the other side is playing political hardball. In 1994, Senate leaders were negotiating over an amendment to the health bill which would protect health insurance for babies. But that didn't stop Democrats from continuing to attack Republicans as insensitive to the needs of children.

That was too much for Dole. "Maybe I haven't been here long enough to understand what I thought was going on. Or maybe I've been here too long."

Unlike Kennedy, Rockefeller, and Mitchell, Bill Clinton does not have a long-standing personal relationship with Dole. Maybe that's why Dole hasn't been quite as tough on him.

Oh, the night Clinton was elected, the angry Dole briefly reappeared, calling Clinton's policy proposals "awful," and asserting that he, Dole, would represent the 57 percent who did not vote for Clinton.

But then a few days later, Dole the conciliator replaced him, even letting the president-elect off the
hook on his commitment to get things done quickly.
"I don't think there's any magic in how much you
do in the first 100 days. If you push to do too much
in too short a time span, you may end up on the reef
somewhere."

Still, for the most part, Dole led his party in opposing *almost* every major Clinton proposal. And on
more than one occasion, this president has been a
victim of the Dole wit. After Clinton proposed his
budget-balancing plan in May of 1995, Dole shot
back, "Since his nonsecret plan didn't get anywhere,
he's going to have a secret plan, which probably
won't get anywhere either."

As to the Republican insistence on balancing the
budget in seven years, as opposed to Clinton's suggested ten years, Dole conjured, or perhaps invented,
an old saying, "There's a saying that's been around
for about as long as America has: That there are two
ways to get to the top of an oak tree. One is to climb.
The other is to find an acorn and sit on it."

CHAPTER TEN

Dole on Republicans

One of the little secrets politicians rarely share is that most of them don't dislike their opponents in the other party nearly so much as their allies in their own party.

It really should come as no surprise. In this country most congressional districts and even some states are pretty safely in the hands of one party. So for lots of congressmen, state legislators, city aldermen, county commissioners, or clerks of the works, the only real opponents are the ones they have to face in primaries. Ambition is more likely to be thwarted by an intraparty foe.

Besides, when you oppose the folks in the other party, it's usually because you disagree with them on the issues. Real politicians don't take issues personally. Often, they don't even take them seriously. Intraparty fighting, among people who agree on most issues, tends to be more personal.

Bob Dole is no exception here. He opposes Democrats. He fights Republicans. He wins some of those fights. He loses others. He forgets none.

Among the Republicans for whom Dole has limited regard is Speaker Newt Gingrich, of whom he once mused, "Sometimes I kind of wonder, 'Well, jimminy, why can't I think like this guy? Is there something wrong with me?' Then I think, 'Well, maybe not.' You can go out there and say, 'I've got nine ideas.' Well, maybe one of them is good. We're the party of ideas, but that doesn't mean every idea is a good idea.

"You hear Gingrich's staff has these five file cabinets, four big ones and one little tiny one. Number one is 'Newt's Ideas.' Number two, 'Newt's Ideas.' Number three, number four—'Newt's Ideas.' The little one is 'Newt's Good Ideas.'"

Later he offered the speaker a Dutch uncle's advice: "I think we all change. It seems to me that when you become Speaker of the House, or even the leader of the Senate, you need to weigh what you say a little more carefully, because somebody is going to interpret it—properly or improperly—and it sometimes has meaning. I think we all have got to be responsible."

Even when he's being a loyal conservative Republican, Dole is not necessarily a *reverent* loyal and conservative Republican. He led the unsuccessful fight to get Judge Robert Bork confirmed to the United States Supreme Court, but not without observing that the acerbic, bewhiskered judge was a tough sell: "The first thing that guy ought to do is shave."

When Dole didn't get picked for the vice presidency in 1988, Senator Dan Quayle did. Quayle immediately got into trouble with allegations that his wealthy, powerful family had helped him get into the National Guard during the Vietnam War. Another Republican senator, John Heinz of Pennsylvania (and of the Heinz ketchup family), quickly praised Quayle. Dole was not impressed, saying of Heinz, "I'll bet he was chauffeured to kindergarten, too."

Quayle was not amused, noting that "remarks like this are one reason Bob Dole has never moved from the Senate to the White House." What Quayle probably didn't know was that the "chauffeured to kindergarten" line was one Dole had often used privately to describe George Bush.

Dole hasn't even always been kind to sitting presidents of his own party. In 1973, Dole was asked if he'd like President Nixon to campaign for him in Kansas the following year. "I'd settle for a flyover in Air Force One."

That later became the standard remark for any senator when the president of his party wasn't doing too well in the polls.

Of Nixon, Dole was a follower, a loyal supporter, a political pupil, but also a shrewd observer. Dole may have equated the ex-president with "evil" that day at the Reagan White House. But that did not prevent him from speaking at Nixon's funeral, ending his talk with this prayer: "May God bless Richard Nixon. And may God bless the United States."

In the 1960s, Dole regularly referred to Nixon as "my president." When Nixon's nomination of Harold Carswell to the United States Supreme Court was in danger, Dole excoriated his fellow Republican senators who were cool to the nomination. Just before the final vote, Dole strode up and down the Senate chamber's center aisle, pointing at individual Republican senators and proclaiming, "I would remind my Republican friends that Richard Nixon was elected president in November 1968, and with that election came the right and duty to nominate justices of the Supreme Court."

Even after the Watergate scandal had become such

a problem for the Republican party that any Republican senator interested in reelection had to be *somewhat* critical of Nixon, Dole hedged his criticism as advice. "Nixon appears to be hiding from the people, who really trust and like him very much."

And when it was revealed that Nixon had been secretly taping all his White House conversations, Dole did not object. He merely joked, "Thank goodness whenever I was in the Oval Office I only nodded."

But his loyalty did not blind him to the flaws in Nixon's White House. "I was very disillusioned with the White House, the arrogant people who worked there. We went through purgatory for a while as a party." White House staffers were, he said, "the gutless wonders who seem to take personal satisfaction in trying to do somebody in."

As it later turned out, Dole was having problems with the Nixon staff even before Watergate. Though he was the Republican national chairman, he couldn't get an appointment to see the president. Finally, he got a phone call from one of the staffers he scorned as "assistant presidents," and as he related it, the conversation went something like this.

"Hey, Bob, do you still want to see the president?"
"When?"
"Tune in on channel nine, he's coming on the tube in ten minutes."

As a loyal Nixon man, Dole could be counted on to attack the president's enemies. But some of the president friends wanted attacks that were too harsh even for Dole. The fiercest of those friends was Charles Colson, who kept sending Dole memos insisting that he link Democratic senators with treason.

According to Jeb Magruder, who discusses the idea in his book *An American Life*, Dole complained to him about it, saying, "I've got one of those Goddamn speeches from Colson. What am I supposed to do? I can't say that stuff."

Magruder suggested that Dole discuss the situation with Attorney General John Mitchell. Dole said, "I talked to Mitchell. He says this Colson speech is junk and I ought to forget it."

When crunch time came, Dole was less loyal to Nixon than he was concerned about his own political survival. When a poll showed that Nixon's approval rating was 26 percent, Dole icily observed, "That's seven degrees below freezing."

Nixon's plummeting authority put the president's supporters in a touchy position. "It's an impossible dilemma. One guy gives me hell for betraying Nixon. The next guy comes up to me and says, 'I'm for you,

Bob, but you've got to get Nixon off your back.' No way to stay on that tightrope for long."

By July of 1974, Dole could see the end in sight. "Everything Nixon touches seems to turn to ashes. But now the trauma is gone. The argument that the country can't stand the strain is no longer a consideration. Fifty-eight to sixty (Senate) votes are already pretty solid for conviction."

By 1974, Gerald Ford was president. Dole was no more enthusiastic. When the new president issued his famed pardon to his predecessor, Dole said he tried to call Ford "to thank him for throwing me an anchor." Asked if he wanted the president's help, Dole answered, "I think Ford's given me about all the help I can stand."

Before Vice President Nelson Rockefeller withdrew from his place on the 1976 Republican ticket, Dole was loyally endorsing his party's leadership—loyally, but not reverentially.

"When he first went in, Ford seemed to have it in the palm of his hand, and then he loses it in a matter of days and he's no great asset to Republican candidates now. Still, if we're going to have a strong, balanced Republican ticket in 1976, we will have to do it with a Ford-Rockefeller ticket. That is if Ford doesn't kick the ball away in the first quarter. He's already fumbled it a couple of times."

None of which means that Dole wasn't delighted to be chosen as Ford's running mate in 1976. Like all the other prospects, he had been waiting by the phone in his Kansas City hotel room. "I didn't expect a call from the president this morning, but I'm glad we were in."

As Dole pointed out, the two men had known each other a long time. "I've known President Ford at a time when I could call him 'Jerry.'"

Actually, there was more to it than that. Ford owed Dole. In 1965, after the Republican debacle under Goldwater, it was Dole who swung four of the five Kansas Republican congressmen behind Ford's bid to become minority leader. That put him over the top.

But even as Ford's running mate, Dole was not above taking a shot at the affable, if sometimes fumbling, top of his ticket. At a speech in San Francisco, an overwrought, anti-union questioner insisted that Dole explain why (in the questioner's view), AFL-CIO chief George Meany was "running the country." Dole couldn't resist: "Well, somebody has to."

Even the politically sainted Ronald Reagan has not been immune from the Dole wrath or the Dole wit, though in this case the uncomplimentary cracks were made in private, the better to avoid enraging the Gipper's many fans. Still, in the confines of his own home or office, Dole could describe Reagan as "a programmed line reader." And as one whose "mind is primitive." And who "thinks in slogans," or even "a befuddled septuagenarian."

Prudence usually kept Dole from making anti-Reagan remarks in public.

Usually. But right after Reagan's landslide reelection in 1984, after a campaign in which the incumbent said very little of substance but did make some vague comments about perhaps making some changes in the tax laws, Dole held up a blank piece of paper before a Florida audience and said, "I've just obtained a copy of President Reagan's secret tax plan."

In 1988, Dole appealed to loyal Reaganites by claiming that when Reagan needed help he called him, not George Bush. But, noted one reporter, when he wanted a running mate in 1980, then he called Bush. Dole shot back, "Did he call collect?"

He showed far less restraint when it came to Reagan's associates, including (especially) Chief of Staff Donald Regan. Discussing the negotiations on the 1985 budget, Dole said, "We can't do it without Ronald Reagan. Maybe we could do it without Don Regan."

Incumbent presidents have not been the only targets of Dole's barbs. One of his rivals for the 1980 Republican nomination was his Senate colleague Howard Baker who is—well—not a tall fellow. When

Baker dropped out of that race, Dole suggested that Baker, "Can always open up a tall men's clothing store—in Japan."

One of his 1988 opponents was Jack Kemp, then a congressman from upstate New York, but once a quarterback for the Buffalo Bills, to whom Dole once said, "You've been playing quarterback too long." And about whom he once said, "There was a certain football player who forgot his helmet and then started talking supply side theory."

Kemp was a supply-sider who championed tax cuts. He was also finely coifed, which inspired Dole to suggest that Kemp was "holding out for a deduction on hair spray."

Another 1988 opponent was Pat Robertson, who claimed to be leading Dole in North Carolina. "He was in Salisbury, North Carolina, about two weeks ago and said I was running second to him. My mother-in-law lives there and she told me. Of course, that's Pat Robertson. He probably gets his bowling results from a different place than I do."

More recently, the major Republican victim of Dole's scorn has been his fellow senator, Phil Gramm of Texas, who wants the same thing Dole does—the 1996 presidential nomination. After Gramm criticized Dole for not supporting a tax cut amendment which Gramm sponsored, and which got beaten, Dole shot back, "I'm the Republican leader, and I guess when you're not part of the leadership, it's easy to make charges. But if I could only produce thirty-one votes for one of my amendments, I wouldn't criticize anybody else. I generally try to win when I offer an amendment."

In June of 1995, Gramm tried to take the lead in stopping the nomination of Dr. Henry Foster as surgeon general. But Dole executed a parliamentary maneuver, and he got the credit for killing the nomination. "We got it done, even though Gramm was out of town."

A month later, the argument was over welfare. Once again, Gramm tried to appear to be the more conservative of the two. Dole was scornful. Anybody, he said, can talk tough. "It's not easy to put together a welfare package. It's easy to put together if you don't care how many votes you get. But to get one that will pass is not easy."

And when Gramm started attacking him almost daily, Dole tried to shrug it off. "If he has to go out and take a shot each day, well, I'm the front-runner."

But no Republican has felt Dole's sting more than George Bush, of whom Dole has said, "He screws with his socks on." And, "I mean, the guy never had to do a day's work in his life." And, "If you can't stand up to Dan Rather, you're going to have problems with Gorbachev and a few other people." And, "He never leaves any footprints, wherever he goes." And, "Maybe he's not in the loop."

That last, of course, was a play on Bush's own explanation about why, even though he was vice president, he didn't really know what was going on when the Reagan Administration sold arms to Iran and used profits to support Nicaraguan rebels.

To say that Dole never quite accepted that would be to understate the case. In fact, he regularly insisted that Bush "should release all his notes and all his memoranda."

And when Bush complained that the press was being unfair to him by asking him about his Iran-Contra role, Dole likened Bush to "sort of the ghost of Spiro Agnew."

Then Bush counterattacked. His campaign staff put out a press release implying (without actually stating) that there was something improper about Mrs. Dole's personal finances.

Dole was furious. "What a cheap shot! What a cheap shot!"

A few days later, he took the unusual step of walking up to Bush as the vice president was presiding over the Senate. Dole held a copy of the Bush campaign's press release in his hand. He approached the big desk in the front of the chamber, and later reported what had occurred. "I asked him, 'Did George Bush authorize this? Did you? I think you owe my wife an apology.'

"Because I couldn't believe that he had authorized this very personal attack on me and my wife, Elizabeth, and I think we—as I told the vice president—*we're running for president!* This is a very important office! And I said, 'Did you authorize this release?'

"He said, 'Yes.'

"I said, 'Did you read it?'

"He said, 'No.'

"And I said, 'Do you know what it contains? Do you know what it says about me and Elizabeth?' I couldn't believe it."

Then Dole threw the copy of the press release onto the desk in front of Bush and said, "Well, *read* it."

Actually, that was not the first time Dole and Bush had clashed on the Senate floor. The other occasion, though, was notable more for its finesse. In 1982, the Republicans were in the uncomfortable position of having to vote to kill the following year's cost-of-living increase for Social Security. Bush's nightmare, and Dole's dream, was that the vote in the Senate would end up a tie, forcing Bush to cast the deciding vote. Dole mused over the possibility, "Don't want George to miss this."

Whether Dole arranged it, or just got lucky, that's the way it happened.

Among those who criticized Dole for that vote was Jack Kemp, who used the issues in the 1988 primaries. Dole shot back, "I know when I watch television my friend, good friend, Jack Kemp's running little ads that Bob Dole has cut your benefits. That's not accurate. But what he didn't tell you in that little ad was that in 1983 when we had the bill up to save Social Security, he voted against it."

CHAPTER ELEVEN

Dole the
Loyal Soldier

So Dole never much liked George Bush. In some ways he never thought much of Ronald Reagan.

But he served them both. Loyally.

Not that he liked everything they did. Not that he helped them do everything they wanted to do. Not, most of all, that he never aimed a wisecrack their way.

But serve them loyally he did. Even when it was hard. "I have some things to get over—New Hampshire, New Orleans. I got roughed up pretty good. I thought they distorted my record in New Hampshire."

This was after Bush was elected, with Dole still the leader of the Republican minority in the Senate. Dole did not try to pretend that Bush was his buddy. "We're different. We have different backgrounds." But, "The race is over. He won. I'm a big boy. I was disappointed. But it's not a question of personalities now. George Bush has nothing but tough decisions ahead of him. We need to circle the wagons and stick together. One thing you can't fail to do is govern. I don't want to look in the rearview mirror."

Still, one thing Dole would not do was advocate any kind of tax increase unless his new president endorsed it first. "I'm still sensitive on that point because of the New Hampshire straddle ad. You won't see any tax increase suggestions coming from this senator."

And there weren't. Dole went along with the 1990 tax increase, but only after Bush had agreed to it. And when Democrats passed another tax hike bill in 1992, Dole stood up for the president's veto. "It's got a lot of tax changes, some would say tax increases. I don't think the president dare sign it."

None of which meant that the Senate leader would never needle his president. At the same time Democrats passed that tax bill (it never did become law), the Congress also passed an energy bill which raised $2.6 billion in higher taxes on certain dangerous chemicals. This one, Dole said, needn't be vetoed. "That's an environmental vote, and he's the environmental president."

And when, that same year, Dole and the Bush Administration had different budget proposals, Dole insisted that the financing methods of his plan "will be legit."

Was that to distinguish his approach from the administration's plan, which relied on new, and perhaps unreliable, accounting methods?

"Right."

Good soldier that he was, Dole had actually *introduced* the president's tax package proposal that year, even though he disagreed with some of it. He didn't like the Democratic alternative, either. "There's not much in either package to really jump-start the economy or blow it out of the water and make it really jump."

Sometimes Dole's metaphors get the better of him.

CHAPTER TWELVE

The Adventures of Congressman Doyle

Sooner or later, and usually sooner, every ambitious young politician learns that he's not as important as he thought he was. Dole learned it in 1961. Unlike most of his colleagues, he delights in telling the tale.

"When I first went to Congress, back in 1961, I learned that you are asked to speak a lot. You may not be any good, just warm and willing, and not even too willing. A little like KP in the army.

"I was asked to go out to Indiana one night, and I was told it was the biggest event in that area in a decade. When I got there, I learned they hadn't had a meeting in ten years.

"I remember going into the terminal, where I met the county chairman, who was in a state of near collapse. He said the advance ticket sales had only reached ten. So he rushed me over to the local radio station to try to hype the sales. He said, 'We're going to cut the tickets from three dollars to one dollar. There's going to be a drawing of a color TV set, and you've got to be present to win, and we're not going to draw 'til Congressman Bob Dole gets through talking.'

"And they started through my bio, which was rather lengthy, since I prepared it myself—born in Kansas, reared in Kansas, wounded in World War II, and on and on and on. We left the studio and got in the car, and about the time we hit the highway, the driver flipped on the radio, and the announcer came on to summarize the interview. He said, 'Congressman Bob Doyle will speak tonight at Legion Hall. Tickets have been slashed to a dollar. Going to be a drawing for a color TV set. You gotta be present to win. We're not going to draw 'til Doyle gets through talking.'

"He said, 'He was born in Kansas, reared in Kansas. Prior to World War II he was a premedical student. He suffered a serious head injury in the war, and then went into politics.''

CHAPTER THIRTEEN

Dole the Candidate

Bob Dole has been good at almost everything.

He was a good student, a superb athlete, a brave soldier. In state and local politics, he never lost a race. He was elected state legislator, county attorney, congressman, and senator. Only once, in 1974, did he even have a close contest. And he won that one, too.

There's only one thing he's done poorly. As a candidate for national office, he's been a bust.

As Gerald Ford's running mate, he did help the ticket carry the farm belt. But his acerbic, uninspiring campaign—especially as seen in the debate with Walter Mondale—may have hurt Ford elsewhere. And he knew it. "I'll never forget the Dole-Mondale debate. And don't think I haven't tried."

Nor was it just the debate. The rest of his campaigning was unimpressive, also. At one point, he was uncharacteristically "Agnewesque," grumbling about unfair press coverage. On the same day he scolded Jimmy Carter for reportedly complaining about *his* press coverage, Dole griped that the *New York Times* was "part of the Carter operation."

In 1980, he dropped out of the presidential race after finishing dead last in the New Hampshire primary. He got 607 votes. He made no excuses. "Obviously, we never got it together. Sometimes I think we should've started earlier."

Later, Dole came up with a theory of what went wrong. He needed the Four *M*s—management, money, media, momentum: "Well, maybe it was five *M*s. I forget the other. I didn't have any of them."

He certainly didn't have a strong enough message. In the candidate debate in Iowa, he said, "If you want a younger Ronald Reagan, I'm here."

It got a laugh, but no votes.

When he tried again eight years later, he did a little better. He won the Iowa precinct caucuses and came in second in New Hampshire.

But second wasn't good enough. "People pay attention to the first of anything. They pay more attention if you're seen as the front runner, so if you stumble in New Hampshire you're dead. Other folks become 'hot.' It's as simple as that."

Money was not his problem in 1988. By the end of 1987, he had raised $9.5 million.

And spent it.

Much of it went to a very expensive campaign headquarters staff in Washington, headed by former Tennessee senator Bill Brock. Brock said he had to spend money to get good people.

Dole's response to his old friend was blunt: "This is eating us alive."

Finding the right people to run his campaigns has always been difficult for Dole, who has been accused of refusing to delegate authority, of insisting on running his own race. "I do delegate, so long as I have competent people. But sometimes it's like turning your life over to a committee. I'll never just say, here's a blank check. I like to know where I'm going before I get on an airplane."

In fact, Dole had hired Brock to begin with because he knew that his political organization may have been political, but wasn't very organized. "I don't know why they send me to one place as opposed to another. There doesn't seem to be any logic to it, or any pattern."

And Dole has always had a problem dealing with political strategists who insist that he outline some grand theme for his candidacy. Once he explained why a big-name campaign strategist wouldn't handle his 1988 effort. "I guess I wouldn't go to the mountaintop and come back with a vision." Another time he said, "We thought about having a vision-of-the-month club just for the media. They'd say, 'That's the wrong vision,' and I'd say, 'That's all right, I got another one.'"

Once, in an Iowa shopping center, Dole noticed a Pearle Vision Center. He said that maybe he'd go in and buy one.

For at least two reasons, losing New Hampshire in 1988 was Bob Dole's own fault.

Reason one? He was politically inept. Twice, he flubbed the taping of television commercials designed to inoculate him against the inevitable attacks against him as insufficiently anti-tax. Dole was supposed to say, "I pledge to veto any attempt by the Democrats to increase the new lower tax rates."

That wasn't as sweeping as the total "no new taxes of any size, shape or form" that was the basis of a "no-tax pledge" being circulated around the state, which some of his opponents were signing. But it might have done the job had he not stumbled over the language. What came out was, "Just let the Democrats try—just let the Democrats try to lower—uh—to scuttle the lower tax rates . . ."

He tried it again at a speech, with a camera crew on hand.

He was awful.

On top of that, he caught front-runneritis. Instead of talking about the real world, he started talking about political strategy, just as George Bush had after *he'd* won the 1980 Iowa caucuses, right before blowing the New Hampshire primary.

Political reporters and the twelve people who listen to those Sunday morning talk shows are interested in strategy. Voters are not. Dole forgot that. Considering how poorly he had done last time, he would say, "If Bob Dole can win in this state, I can be president. That's how important it is."

Reason two? He was intellectually honest.

In the final preprimary debate, the Sunday evening before the voting, one of the also-ran candidates, former Delaware governor Pierre "Pete" duPont, reached into his pocket and took out a copy of the no-tax "pledge."

Now, at this point, something should be understood. Taxes are not overwhelmingly popular anywhere. But they are singularly unpopular in New Hampshire, which has no "broad-based" sales or income tax. Tourists pay hotel and meals taxes. Cigarettes and liquor are taxed and the state rakes in revenues from dog and horse tracks situated right near the Massachusetts line. Furthermore, some towns and cities have rather high property-tax rates. Those are the towns and cities where the children actually learn things in their schools.

But there are no other taxes, and the citizens of New Hampshire, especially the Republican citizens, and most especially the *conservative* Republican citizens are very, very finicky about keeping it that way. They don't like taxes at *all*. And they're the ones who vote in primaries.

So it was not a bad little ploy for Pete duPont to pull out this pledge document and to shove it in the lap of the fellow who was sitting immediately to his left.

Dole.

"Sign it," duPont said.

Dole took the few pages of the "pledge," handling it as though he thought it were something duPont had lifted out of the gutter. He gave it a puzzled look and said, "Give it to George. I have to read it first."

Well, in and of itself, that little comment might not have been such a big deal.

It wasn't in and of itself.

That very weekend, the Bush campaign had begun to run a very tough commercial—thereafter enshrined in political folklore as the "straddle" ad, which charged, "Bob Dole straddles, and he just won't promise not to raise taxes."

Unlike so many political commercials, this one was absolutely honest. Dole would not so promise.

Nor would he sign the "pledge," a decision he later half-regretted. "I thought I'd just take the thing and sign it. But then you're in the same class as everybody else. Do anything to get elected. You couldn't even close loopholes under that pledge. I wondered about whether I should have signed that thing."

This time, he didn't quit after New Hampshire. He and his aides thought that things couldn't get worse.

They were wrong.

The next big test was in the South, where several states held their primaries on the same "Super Tuesday." It was while Dole was campaigning in Florida that the simmering dissension between his long-time campaign aides and the newcomers brought in by Brock broke into the open. Brock flew from Washington to Florida to fire two of Dole's oldest political associates—conservative strategists David Keene and Don Devine, who were riding with Dole on his campaign plane, dubbed by the press corps as "the plane from hell."

When Brock told Dole what he was about to do, the candidate made a brief, feeble effort to protect his old friends. "They're just trying to help."

But he couldn't very well countermand the decision of the very guy he had put in charge of the organization. Not after all those newspaper stories about how he had been afraid to delegate in the past. He had delegated to Brock. Now he had to stick with him. When Keene went to see Dole, all Dole could say was, "I'll see you back in Washington. I need your help. I guess that's how it has to be."

Keene asked how he should explain this to the press. The candidate answered, "Gingerly."

But it's hard to be ginger when two top campaign aides and their suitcases are left on the tarmac of the Orlando Airport.

Super Tuesday was a wipeout, and Dole really knew his campaign was over, but he limped on to Illinois. There, he decided to bet everything on a last-minute, live television extravaganza from Knox College in downstate Galesburg. From what he said to his media consultant, Mike Murphy, it seems clear that he knew he couldn't win, but that he wanted to lose with grace. "Look, I know it's tough. I'm not asking you to do anything easy. But we're thirty points behind, and if I'm going to go down the tubes, I'd at least rather go down doing something."

Six minutes and thirty seconds through the program, the television picture went out. Dole kept talking, but then the producers cut him off and started running a segment of his campaign video biography. It was a disaster.

At the time, the Dole operatives tried to console themselves, and their candidate, that Bush would lose the election, and that Dole would be anointed by the press as "the front-runner for '92." He wasn't too consoled. "Yeah, and that's how old I'll be."

Part of Dole's problem as a national candidate is that both times, he ran for president while remaining as his party's leader in the Senate. This, he acknowledged, can be a problem. "I guess it's hard to give two jobs 100 percent. Maybe I've been too cautious.

You can't generate any money if you're not out there. Maybe I'm my own worst enemy."

In some ways, Dole has always been mystified by the peculiarities of presidential campaigns. "Is this how you get the nomination, ninety-nine visits to one place? It's like dipping in the ocean with a teaspoon. So you see three hundred people, or four hundred, or you had one-on-ones. There are only 300 million more people to see. Perhaps there's a better way to do it."

And in fighting for the Republican nomination, Dole's reputation as a conciliator, a careful legislator, has been less an advantage than a problem. The ideological conservatives aren't impressed by his legislative accomplishments, as he has acknowledged.

"I think they're looking for a cheerleader. My view is that leadership is more important than cheerleading.

"I think if there's a complaint, it comes from people who don't understand, first of all, leadership, and secondly, the Senate. You're not 'cutting deals'; you're out there trying to get something done."

CHAPTER FOURTEEN

Dole and Ideology

`` If you're looking for ideology—well, there's Ronald Reagan. Then you see how the debt went up during those years."

That was no liberal Democrat. It was Bob Dole, talking early in 1995, shortly after his party, campaigning on a conservative "Contract with America," took control of Congress. Dole was not all that impressed.

"If you look back at 1994, people say it was won because of the Contract with America. Well, surveys show—what?—10, 12 percent of voters knew what it was all about. The American people were voting for change, just as I assume they were voting for change in 1992. If anybody could tell me precisely what the message was, I'll eat their hat."

It isn't that Dole has no ideology. He does. He's a conservative.

But there's a difference between having an ideology and being an ideologue. An ideologue subjects *all* issues to his ideological test. Dole doesn't do that. So on some issues he's more of a moderate than a conservative.

And on a few issues, at least some of the time, Dole's positions are even—dare one say?—liberal.

Even a bit of a bleeding heart. "It's really sad. You drive home. You see the people on the street, the homeless people. Well, you can't let your emotions dictate everything. But you have to be at least a little bit sensitive.

"I am trying to impress my Republican friends that we are not anti-people. We Republicans are always reacting to these programs. It seems time now for us to be responsive to people who are eligible and who are not being adequately served."

Even in his early days, when he was such a smoldering, angry partisan that some of his fellow Republicans found him annoying (one said he "couldn't sell beer on a troop ship"), Dole was more of an operational conservative than an ideological conservative.

The GOP then was divided between Eisenhower conservatives who acknowledged that there were problems, but were reluctant to prescribe government solutions, and the Goldwater conservatives, who often denied that the problems existed at all.

Dole tended toward the Eisenhower viewpoint. So

that while he voted against the creation of Medicare back in 1965 when he was still in the House, he did so somewhat reluctantly. "The real opposition to the bill stems from the fact (that) hospitalization benefits are to be financed by a compulsory payroll tax administered by the Social Security Administration. The point is that nearly everyone supports the concept that adequate medical protection should be made available to the aged, but it should be voluntary and should reflect ability to pay."

And though Dole is conservative, he finds it hard to be reverent about all the conservative icons. He usually supports the Pentagon's spending requests. But he has also referred to it as "that sandbox across the river."

And though his voting record is strongly pro-business, he has occasionally referred to corporate lobbyists as "advocates for the truly greedy."

Dole calls himself "fairly consistently conservative on the economic side, foreign policy side, defense side."

But Senate leaders can't be down-the-line ideologues. And Dole isn't.

CHAPTER FIFTEEN

Dole the Liberal

Well, relatively speaking.
Dole is liberal in relation to:

- some other Republicans
- some of Bob Dole

Or, to put it another way, Dole is a conservative with a few liberal instincts. Some of these stem from his low-income childhood, some from his own physical handicap, and some from his experience in government, which, unlike many conservatives, he does not oppose. "The government," he once noted, "does a lot of good."

And he meant the federal government.

In some circles, you can get run out of town for that.

But Dole remembers his background. His first

elected office was as Russell County attorney. "I had to take children away from their parents. I had to approve the welfare documents, the checks for my grandparents, who were poor. That left a very strong imprint that there are a lot of people out there who are desperate. A lot of these people who cry out for help really need it. They're not just cheats."

Often, Dole tries to suppress this kind of talk, usually at the urging of his political advisors, who keep reminding him that Republican audiences really aren't interested in hearing it. But he doesn't always do what he's told.

Campaigning for the Republican presidential nomination in 1988, Dole came upon a very white, very comfortable crowd in Gwinnett County, Georgia, smack dab in Newt Gingrich's district, and rejected the advice of his handlers thusly: "I think we also have to be sensitive to the needs of a lot of people out there—some in this area—who may be white, some may be black, some may be brown, some may be poor and old, or poor and young, or disabled. What we call vulnerable groups in America sometimes need a helping hand . . . sometimes they can't find help. So what are you going to do? I hope you'd agree, there's a responsibility for the federal government to step in."

On more than one occasion, Dole has made certain

that the federal government did step in. He co-sponsored creation of the Consumer Protection Agency, and he has quietly protected several federal food and nutrition programs for the poor.

In 1981, when Ronald Reagan's energetic new administration was determined to slash social spending, Dole spoke up during a meeting with the president: "Somebody else is going to have to start taking hits besides welfare recipients."

On another occasion that year, he complained about some corporate lobbyists pushing for cuts in social spending. "They almost beat the homeless, and now they're after the senior citizens."

With Dole, it is important to remember, what you hear is not always what you get. There are times when he talks like a true conservative, but quietly helps enact policies more attuned to Ted Kennedy than to Jesse Helms.

In the budget debate of 1987, for instance, Dole rose on the Senate floor to object to some proposed health spending, including expansion of Medicaid's prenatal care, as "just another instance of how Congress puts spending on automatic pilot."

Later, in private, he told liberal Democratic Representative Henry Waxman of California not to take him literally and to press ahead with the program. It became law, thanks to Bob Dole, who had spoken against it.

On April 14, 1969, Dole rose for his maiden speech as a United States senator, and this one was not about the Communist menace or the spendthrift ways of the Democrats. Instead, he spoke of the "exceptional group which I joined on another April 14, twenty-four years ago, a minority group whose existence affects every person in our society and the very fabric of our nation."

Dole said his minority—the handicapped—"has always known exclusion. Maybe not exclusion from the front of the bus, but perhaps from even climbing aboard it; maybe not exclusion from pursuing advanced education, but perhaps from experiencing any formal education; maybe not exclusion from day-to-day life itself, but perhaps from an adequate opportunity to develop and contribute to his or her fullest capacity."

To help handicapped people become economically self-sufficient, Dole founded the Dole Foundation. It raised $9.5 million for its work between 1988 and 1994.

As always with Dole, there is a political motive at work here. He thinks that in the long run, Republicans can win over some of the less fortunate if they show a bit of sensitivity toward them, and he has often said so.

"I don't find many people in wheelchairs showing up at our meetings. We have got to be sensitive to the so-called vulnerable groups—people who can't fend for themselves. They could be senior citizens. They could be poor. They could be children. They could be handicapped. We've got to be seen as being as sensitive to these groups as the Democrats.

"I don't see this as conservative or liberal or moderate. I see this as a sensible and proper thing we ought to focus on."

That prenatal health care bill was not the only time Dole didn't just talk like a liberal, but acted like one, too. He and Democratic senator Robert Byrd of West Virginia co-sponsored a law to help the homeless. And in 1983, Dole played a key role on the committee which restructured, and preserved, the Social Security program. He likes to tell how it happened.

"We fixed it. Ronald Reagan appointed a commission, and Tip O'Neill, the Speaker, a Democrat, was on it. And Senator Pat Moynihan, a Democrat, was on it. And Bob Dole was on it. We were stalemated, and one day I said to Pat Moynihan on the Senate floor, I said, 'Pat, we've got to give this just one more try.' I said, 'You know, some people don't have anything else except their Social Security.' So we gave it another try, and we fixed it, and Social Security is going to be in good shape at least until the year 2017, and probably beyond."

Dole has not said much about gays. It's a touchy subject for a conservative Republican, unless he's going to attack the notion of gay rights. Dole isn't about to do that, which probably explains his tendency simply to ignore the subject. But in a 1995 interview with the *New York Times Magazine*, he did say, "Well, you watch some of these programs. You read some of the material and you say, well, they don't have any choice. Something else happens. Somewhere in the genes, or whatever. I don't know whether it's involuntary or choice. But either way they have, obviously, civil rights. No discrimination. That is America."

For years, one of the liberals who all right-thinking conservatives loved to hate was George McGovern. Dole blasted McGovern with the best of them when the South Dakota senator ran against Richard Nixon in 1972. But the two men—World War II veterans from the Great Plains—liked each other. In 1980, when a conservative group wanted Dole to sign an anti-McGovern fund-raising letter, he wouldn't do it. Later he explained, "The language was too offensive."

They even worked together on legislation to improve the food stamp program. Dole likes food stamps for two reasons: they help poor people eat and they help Kansas farmers sell grain. Either way, Dole makes no apologies. "Some say, 'Well, he supported food stamps.' My view is, that's too bad.

There's a need. I worked with George McGovern on it. That's an indictment. I don't agree with McGovern on much, but on this we found common ground."

In 1975, when Dole and McGovern were trying to liberalize the program, Senator James Buckley, the conservative New Yorker, was trying to make it tougher for people to get food stamps. At one Senate hearing, Dole put this question to his colleague: "Do you put in a burial allowance, for the ones who starve?"

CHAPTER SIXTEEN

Dole the Moderate

As a good conservative Bob Dole doesn't think the federal government should do much. "Let me repeat what Ronald Reagan said a few years ago, because it fits this day: 'In this present crisis, government is not the solution to our problems. Government is the problem.' It's called the message. Limited government. Rein in the federal government."

But not always.

Not, sometimes, when it comes to helping the very poor. Dole voted against Lyndon Johnson's antipoverty program. But in 1974, when the Nixon Administration wanted to demolish it, he voted against that, too.

And when the Republicans took power in 1981, he said, "Now that we Republicans have some responsibility, we have to be very careful before we just go

113

along with people taking off after programs and saying there is no need for them."

And not when it comes to racial discrimination.

Dole is against it. He's so against it he thinks it should be against the law.

Federal law.

"There oughtn't to be discrimination. Everything ought to be based on potential. Everyone should be treated alike, whether they're black or brown or disabled or homosexual."

Dole might not be a full-blown racial liberal. He's always had qualms about affirmative action, and he's been as quick as anyone to attack some of the more bizarre methods of racial protest. But he could be called a four-square racial moderate. The lard-line conservatives fought the move to make Martin Luther King, Jr's. birthday a national holiday. Dole cosponsored it. He also voted for the constitutional amendment (never ratified by the states), which would have given full voting rights to the District of Columbia and its black majority.

And when many Republicans, including George Bush's White House, were trying to use the "quota" issue against the 1991 Civil Rights Bill, Dole quietly helped his Republican colleague John Danforth shepherd the bill through the Senate.

First of all, he thought it was good politics. "From a party standpoint, it was not in our interest to get locked in. We had to bring everybody along fairly slowly; we had a few in our party who thought that would be a great issue, we shouldn't drop it."

The "great issue" he was talking about was the quota issue. Some Republicans wanted to keep it in the headlines. Dole wanted to pass a bill. He kept pushing the White House and Danforth to work out language, and ultimately he endorsed the compromise, calling it, "Not the grab-bag approach advocated by the Beltway interest groups and the lawyers' lobby (but) the only way out of the civil rights quagmire without producing quotas."

And while Dole may believe in conservative policies, he's an advocate (and a practitioner) of prudent processes. "I don't think you want to leave people in the audience thinking you're some radical that's going to take them over the edge."

There is another reason Dole is sometimes considered less than conservative.

That reason? He's a real conservative—the old fashioned kind—the kind who believes in balanced budgets.

According to this traditional conservatism (and traditional liberalism, for that matter), there are but three ways to balance a budget:

1. spend less money
2. raise less money
3. some combination of 1 and 2

Along about the late 1970s, there emerged a new

kind of conservative, proclaiming Option (4), based on a new kind of arithmetic which held that the government could raise *more* money by *lowering* tax rates.

This is known as supply side economics. Dole never bought it. "The good news is, a bus full of supply-siders went over a cliff last night. The bad news is, there were three empty seats."

Supply side theory holds that lower taxes will inspire more economic activity, and will therefore lead to *higher* tax revenues even with a *lower* tax rate. History shows that this actually works.

Sometimes.

Dole is one of those who worries about the times it won't work. And while he likes low tax rates as much as the next guy (unless he's standing next to Jack Kemp or Newt Gingrich), he worries about the deficit. "I've grown up in this party fighting deficits. I happen to believe they will have a negative impact."

And he's convinced the government needs *some* money, as long as it has to run an army, an interstate highway system, and the national parks. "People who advocate only cutting taxes live in a dream world. We Republicans have been around awhile. We don't have to march in lockstep with the supply-siders."

In 1990, Dole went along with George Bush's tax increases, even though they enraged the supply-siders. "Some of my colleagues say, 'Why are you up there doing this? You ought to be out there with us: No New Taxes.' But I'm the leader. I'm the Republican leader. I'm not Newt Dole, you know."

No, he wasn't. When it came down to a choice between supporting his president and supporting the rebels in his own party, Dole the governing insider and Dole the deficit-cutter won out easily. "I don't think you can duck it. Somebody is going to have to do it one of these days. This deficit is building and building and building, and it's going to explode all over everybody."

Besides, it was long before 1990 that Gingrich and the supply-siders had given Dole the title "tax collector for the welfare state."

That happened in 1982. A year earlier, Ronald Reagan's first as president, the Republicans passed what they called the biggest tax cut in history. Dole, as chairman of the Senate Finance Committee, played a major role in passing it.

With one exception, the tax cut was a big success. The exception was that the federal deficit got bigger. A lot bigger.

When it threatened to get bigger yet the next year, Dole went into action, concocting a complex tax bill that closed some corporate loopholes and instituted a "minimum tax" on wealthy companies and individuals who benefited from various tax preferences.

The supply-siders, in Congress and the White House, were furious. "What they tried to get me to do was to abandon principle. I said, 'If you'll just let me amend it so I can put in that you can close loopholes.' They said, 'Nope, that would be a tax increase for a company.' I said, 'Well, that's crazy.' But, oh no, you gotta be Simon pure. You can't raise anybody's taxes."

It wasn't that Dole did not also propose spending cuts. For instance, he suggested trimming the fees some doctors, including pathologists, were billing to Medicare. This angered some of them. "A pathologist in Kansas offered to give me a free autopsy. The trouble is, he wants to do it now."

Dole also angered some of the corporate lobbyists by not letting them into all his Finance Committee sessions. "There they are, lined up Gucci to Gucci. They'll all be barefoot by morning."

One of Dole's revenue-raising suggestions was to require restaurant owners to estimate, and withhold, some of the tip income of their employees. The restaurant owners lobbied against this so strenuously, that even though the provision was in the bill when it came out of Dole's committee, the full Senate knocked it out.

The restaurant lobbyists were delighted. They had outsmarted Bob Dole on Senate procedure.

Guess again, guys. Senate rules prevented any individual senator, even Dole, from offering an amendment that had not been considered by the committee. But Dole had been around. He got the parliamentarian to agree that the committee itself could offer an amendment. Dole polled his members, and—voila!— there appeared an amendment which would have made it much tougher for businessmen to deduct their expensive restaurant lunches. Dole explained his logic: "If you can't take the income out of the restaurants, then you can just take the customers out of them."

They made a deal. The restaurants agreed to the withholding provision; Dole dropped the deduction limit. By mid-summer, Dole had even persuaded Reagan to support his tax bill, and it passed, with the help of several liberal Democrats.

But Reagan's support did not mollify the committed supply-siders, and Dole knew it. "I'm perceived as a moderate Republican for all the work I've done on tax reform, voting rights, food stamps, all the stuff for veterans and the handicapped."

But it isn't so much that Dole is a moderate as that he's not an ideologue. He's a pragmatist, and he's proud of it. "If you've got a problem out there and you can solve 90 percent of it by making modifications or you can solve none of it by being hard-nosed about it, I think most Americans are looking at results, not how far out somebody can position themselves along the political spectrum. Bob Dole is a conservative who gets things done."

CHAPTER SEVENTEEN

Dole the Conservative

Make no mistake, though: at heart, Bob Dole is a conservative.

First of all, he says he is. "My credentials are good. I'm more flexible than some would like. I like to work things out. Some of them would rather lose than compromise. But I'm right on the issues. I voted for prayer in the schools. I voted for the anti-abortion amendment. I voted for the balanced budget amendment."

And he's not going to let anyone "out-conservative" him without a fight. "I'm perceived as a moderate Republican for all the work I've done on tax reform, voting rights, food stamps, all the stuff for veterans and the handicapped. But we're going to make a play for the conservatives. I think I deserve a shot at them."

In other words, Dole is saying, all those exceptions to his conservatism are . . . well, exceptions.

He's right. To find his liberal or moderate sentiments, one has to go looking, sometimes deep into the past, or in interviews given in unusually pensive moods.

The conservative statements hit you right in the face. Just pick your issue.

Family and medical leave? "We have no idea just how much it will cost business. We are talking about tens of thousands of jobs being lost or not created because of this bill."

Or, "I don't want anyone to have the impression we're holding up the Family Leave Act, although I wouldn't mind doing just that."

The Motor Voter bill? "When Big Brother in Washington slaps an unfunded mandate on the states, somebody has to pay the bill for the federal edict."

The National Endowment for the Arts and the Public Broadcasting Service? "We spend hundreds of millions of dollars on the endowments for the arts and humanities. Why is the federal government in the culture business? In this explosion of the information age, why do we have a Corporation for Public Broadcasting?"

Lyndon Johnson's Great Society? "There are more people living in poverty today than before the Great Society Started."[2]

---

[2]Not so. There were 38 million poor people, 17.8 percent of the population, in 1963, only 36.9 million at last count, and that was only 11.6 percent. The low point for poverty came during the Carter Administration.

Affirmative action? Well, he's been for it in the past. But that was the "old" new Dole. The "new" new Dole (the newer Dole?) says, "Affirmative action is another federal policy out of control. Discrimination is wrong. Discrimination is immoral. This is America. We should have a color-blind society, but fighting discrimination should never be used to divide Americans by race, ethnic background, or gender."

On this issue, Dole had no choice but to acknowledge publicly that he had changed his position. Introducing what he called the "Equal Opportunity Act of 1995," he said, "For too many of our citizens, our country is no longer the land of opportunity, but a pie chart where jobs and other benefits are often awarded not because of hard work or merit but because of someone's biology.

"Now I have an admission to make. While I have questioned and opposed group preferences in the past, I have also supported them. That's my record, and I am not hiding from it.

"But many of us who supported these policies never imagined that preferences would become a seemingly permanent fixture in our society."

Though he has often supported programs designed to help the poor, Dole took the lead in sponsoring a generally conservative welfare bill in 1995. For some

Republicans, though, notably his presidential rival Senator Phil Gramm, it wasn't conservative enough.

They wanted strict rules about who could qualify for welfare. Dole wanted to leave most of those decisions to the states, a policy he described as "the key to true conservative reform."

Typically, Dole was unable to resist having a little fun with the issue. So he pointed out that his "state's rights" approach had won the supports of the governors of Texas, New Hampshire, Iowa, and Arizona, "to name a few early primary states."

Seconds later he made it clear that "this is not about presidential politics."

And now, in his latest conservative incarnation, Dole is edging close to the supply-siders. "Let me make one fundamental belief crystal clear. We can cut taxes and balance the budget all at the same time. Middle-class families are forced to send too much of their hard-earned money to Washington. We should provide a tax credit to children and remove the marriage penalty to strengthen our families."

So it should be no surprise that on his first trip to New Hampshire in 1995, Dole did what he wouldn't do in 1988—he signed an anti-tax pledge.

There is another new aspect to Dole's conservatism. Taking a cue from some of the Western conservatives who oppose federal environmental regulations (Dole had a zero rating in 1994 from the League of Conservation Voters), Dole is trying to revive interest in, and strict adherence to, the Tenth Amendment to the Constitution.

"My mandate as president would be to rein in the federal government in order to set free the spirit of the American people; to reconnect our government in Washington with the common sense values of our citizens; and to reassert American interests wherever and whenever they are challenged around the world. My guide in this would be the final piece of the Bill of Rights—the Tenth Amendment."

In almost every speech, Dole proceeds to quote the amendment, saying, "The powers not delegated to the United States by the Constitution . . . are reserved to the states, or to the people."

Actually, he misquotes it. In full (and sometimes he does quote it in full), it reads: "The powers not delegated to the United States, nor prohibited by it to the states, are reserved to the states respectively, or to the people."

Whether his minor misquotation changes the meaning of the amendment is not clear, because neither is the meaning of the amendment. A unanimous United States Supreme Court once called the Tenth Amendment "but a truism that all is retained which has not been surrendered."

Nor does Dole seem to recognize that all this Tenth Amendment talk holds some political peril. After all, the Constitution does not specifically empower the federal government to operate a Social Security System, to maintain the National Parks, to send Commodity Credit checks to farmers or to build highways. In fact, when Social Security was first passed, opponents used the Tenth Amendment to try to argue that it was unconstitutional.

As it has for most of this century, the Supreme Court ruled that the constitutional provision empowering Congress to regulate interstate commerce "is complete in itself, may be exercised to its utmost extent, and acknowledges no limitations other than are prescribed in the Constitution."

But to Dole, the meaning of the Tenth Amendment is plain: "The federal government should do only those things specifically called for in the Constitution. All others should remain with the states or the people. It is a philosophy of freedom conceived in liberty, tested by history, yet all too often ignored in Washington. I intend to restore it."

Specifically, he says, "We will roll back federal programs, laws and regulations from A to Z—from Amtrak to zoological studies—working our way through the alphabet soup of government. Our guide will be this question: Is this program a basic function of a limited government, or is it an example of how government has lost faith in the judgments of our people and the potential of our markets?"

What would be cut?

"With the exception of Social Security, every bureaucracy and bureaucrat, every government program and federal expense, is ripe for reduction and elimination.''

Dole has also adopted some of the foreign policy views of the most conservative Republicans, including antipathy toward the United Nations. "We must stop placing the agenda of the United Nations before the interests of the United States. When we take our revolution to the White House in 1996, we will vow that American policies will be determined by us, not by the United Nations. Let us remember that America has been the greatest force for good the world has ever known.''

One issue on which Dole's conservatism has never wavered is abortion. He came into public life against it, and he's still against it.

Surprisingly, though, he hasn't *said* much about it, except to say that he's against it. Dole takes the anti-abortion position on all Senate votes, he is on record as favoring the abortion-banning "Human Life Amendment" to the Constitution, and he calls himself "pro-life." But it is not an issue he stresses, nor is it one he discusses very much. His position is, as he has said, "unambiguous," but it seems more visceral than philosophical, which perhaps is why he often proclaims it but rarely articulates it.

Here again though, Dole is reliably conservative; he is not an ideologue. Unlike some of his allies on this issue, he would allow abortions when pregnancies resulted from rape or incest, or if the life of the pregnant woman were endangered. Furthermore, to the consternation of some anti-abortion true believers, he refused to say that if he wins the presidential nomination he will choose only an anti-abortion running mate.

That would be, he said, "like saying you are not going to have anybody who is left-handed or right-handed."

And in the summer of 1995, Dole again refused to sign a "pledge," this one affirming the rights of the unborn child. When asked about it, he said, "This campaign is about replacing Bill Clinton, not making cynical predictions about how to 'play' abortion as an issue. We'll leave that to other campaigns."

Though a conservative, Dole is not one of the ultra-libertarians who became so powerful when Republicans took control of Congress in 1994. He believes in limited government. But he is still not anti-government.

"What I want to do is to reconnect the government with the American people—the average American out there—make it more user-friendly. We want to rein in the government, make it more responsive. It's become too intrusive."

CHAPTER EIGHTEEN

Dole on the Issues

One of the problems with being a senator is that you have to have a position on every issue.

It's a political disability.

Governors have it easy. Outside their own states, hardly anybody knows how they stand on any issues, *except the ones they want to highlight.*

So that, for instance, everyone who cares knows these days where Governor Pete Wilson of California stands on immigration and affirmative action.

Quick: Where is he on health care and education?

Who knows?

In fact, who can find out?

Well, you *can* find out. But it isn't easy.

With senators, though, it's a piece of cake. They all have these voting records.

For Senate leaders, it's even easier. They've usually

been seen on TV holding forth about whichever issue is being debated. They can't hide.

Dole, who has been part of the Senate leadership for at least twenty years, has an abundantly clear record on most issues.

This doesn't mean he's been a leader, or even a debater, on every issue. His Senate leadership has come largely through his work on the Finance Committee. That committee has a broad mandate, but it doesn't cover everything. There isn't much in the Dole record on education, for instance, or on the environment. At least not until 1995. Then he sponsored a bill (it didn't pass) which would have gutted environmental regulations in the name of "regulatory reform."

Nor does his extensive record mean that Dole has always been on the same side of every issue. As previously noted, he's changed his mind here and there. Still, it's a fairly consistent record, and a very full one. So full that any accounting of it has to be somewhat selective.

Herewith a selection.

CAMPAIGN FINANCE AND CONGRESSIONAL REFORM

Like most Republicans, Dole opposes putting limits on how much a candidate can spend. "Often, the only way a challenger can compete with the built-in advantages of incumbency is to spend money. The bottom line is that spending limits are designed to prevent change at a time when the American people are demanding change."

In May of 1993, Dole voted for the bill that would have outlawed almost all gifts to senators from lobbyists. When a similar bill came up for a vote in 1994, he said, "We're prepared to correct all the abuses, real or perceived, that have tarnished the credibility of Congress. We're prepared to deal with the gifts portion right now."

But he voted no. He explained that he had not read the measure carefully enough the first time.

He was similarly unenthusiastic about the gift ban idea the following year, warning his colleagues against "going over the cliff here in our efforts to make sure we are all Simon pure."

Besides, he said, "If you don't have any friends and they don't give you any gifts, then you don't have a problem."

Like almost all Republicans, Dole voted against that 1994 lobbying bill the second time around because the GOP had decided that it would have required any citizen who joined an organization that lobbied the Congress to be identified. "When we talk about grass roots lobbying, we're not talking about high-priced lobbyist lunches or legislative deals; we're talking about activity out there in America, when the people band together to let their elected representatives know where they stand on the issues that affect them."

Actually, the bill would not have done what the Republicans said it would. But they beat it anyway.

In one private conversation, Dole offered the ultimate (and sometimes accurate) refutation of the charge that the fat cats who make big contributions always get their way with politicians. Sometimes, Dole said, the best thing to do with big contributors is to "take their money and screw 'em."

HEALTH CARE

Here again, Dole has altered his sentiments. In 1993, he seemed to be as committed to the idea of universal coverage as was Bill Clinton. "I think we start off saying, 'OK, let's try to have universal coverage.' It may take a while. The Clinton plan says 1997. We say the year 2000. Who knows what it is going to be?"

But those were details. The need, he said, was clear: "If you can't get health care, you've got problems."

He even expressed admiration for Hillary Clinton's knowledge of health care complexities. "You don't pick it up on the way home." But he added, "We'll see when we disagree—and we'll disagree."

After Clinton made his major health care address in 1993, Dole was cooperative. "We can have bipartisanship."

By the summer of 1994, though, Dole was explaining that he didn't really mean to insist on universal coverage. "I think I agreed that was certainly a goal. I didn't object to everybody being covered. But I did object on how we were going to do it, and how we were going to get there and how they defined it."

There were no doubt several reasons for Dole's change of heart, but one seemed to be that he didn't think his offer of bipartisanship had been reciprocated. "We thought we were going to be consulted on health care and we haven't heard zip.

"Why aren't we sitting together? Why don't we make a list of all the things we agree on? We can go in a back rom and in two or three days get a bill that could pass 99 to 1."

In a reflective moment, though, Dole candidly wondered whether he would have acted very differently were he in Clinton's place. "I'm trying to be objective. What would we do if we had the majority in Congress and the White House? Would we care what the other party thought? I think we might."

But maybe, he acknowledged, they might not.

For all his anger at Clinton's tactics, as late as May of 1994, Dole was still working to get some kind of bill passed. On the plane ride back from Richard Nixon's funeral in California, he dragged six sleepy members of Congress to a 1 a.m. meeting in the VIP cabin of their military plane.

A few weeks later, though, Dole was ridiculing the notion that there was a "health crisis" in the country. "If you want to see a health care crisis, go to Sarajevo, or go somewhere in Rwanda. We don't have a crisis in America."

And he swiftly counterattacked White House complaints: "One day they attack me. The next day they attack employers. The next day it's insurance companies. It's politics as usual at the White House. They are looking for enemies instead of solutions."

For a while, he supported Republican Senator John Chafee's bill, which would have required every individual to get health insurance, and provided some subsidies.

Then he changed his mind.

In the end, he denounced all the Democrats' plans as examples of "a massive overdose of government control."

And he celebrated the demise of health care reform in 1994. "The bottom line is that instead of wondering what went wrong with this debate, the White House should wake up and realize that a lot went right."

He still agreed, however, that "there's nothing worse than being unable to afford health care for yourself and your family. Republicans know very well there are people in need, and Republicans want to help."

FOREIGN POLICY

Like all political pros, Dole knows that while what happens overseas may be genuinely important, its political impact is minimal unless it affects people at home. "If you ask people about foreign policy, their eyes glaze over. They don't really care. But if something happens where we play some critical role, then the American people care."

Dole has been, by and large, a hawk.

For a while, in 1987, he was more hawkish than Ronald Reagan. When Reagan and Soviet leader Mikhail Gorbachev agreed to a treaty to regulate medium-range nuclear weapons, Dole did not immediately endorse Senate ratification. His first reaction was "I don't trust Gorbachev."

And when America's European friends *did* endorse it quickly, Dole wondered whether the administration was "stuffing this treaty down the throats of the allies."

Ultimately, he did endorse it.

For most of the 1980s, Dole had little to say about Central America. But after visiting Nicaragua in 1987, when the Sandinistas were still in charge, he came up with this solution: "a little three-day invasion."

When critics called that an irresponsible statement, Dole insisted he was "just giving an opinion."

He played a more centrist role in the political crisis in the Philippines. He was one of the Republicans who supported democracy, and after the newly (and truly) elected Philippine president, Corazon Aquino, spoke to a joint session of Congress, Dole said to her, "Cory, you just hit a home run."

She knew what he meant. They play baseball in

the Philippines and she said, "I hope the bases were loaded."

He votes to give the Pentagon most of what it asks and has backed all U.S. military actions abroad.

Except the one in Haiti.

There he demanded "certification" of American interests before committing troops. "We haven't sent them yet to Haiti. So let us speak before it happens."

Before sending American troops into combat in Kuwait, he had expressed no such hesitation. "I do believe that our best chance for peace and the best hope for peace is to strengthen the president's hand in every way we can."

Not that he was a slavish supporter of George Bush's policies. Bush tried to argue that he didn't need congressional approval to go to war in the Gulf. Dole disagreed.

"For months we have been standing on the sidelines, making all kinds of speeches, but not casting a single vote. Congress has been AWOL.

"In my view, if we could ever get it to a vote in the Senate—because there we have unlimited debate, you'd have to shut off debate, that takes sixty votes—but if we could get it to a vote, I think it would pass with a bipartisan majority."

But he had little patience for those who wanted to give the Iraqis more time.

"No more stalls, no more double talk—it's time for action.

"Let's not pull the rug out from under the president when the pressure is building on Saddam Hussein by the minute. Let's don't give him any relief."

And here, as everywhere, he could be caustic about the Democrats who differed with a Republican president. "The Republican strategy is to get Saddam Hussein out of Kuwait. Some of the Democrats' strategy appears to be to get Bush out of the White House."

And after the war's successful conclusion, when many Republicans thought (incorrectly, it turned out) that Democrats who had voted against the president would be vulnerable the following year, Dole eagerly joined the effort to turn the military victory against the Democrats. A mere shift of three votes in the Senate, he wrote, "could have turned this smashing victory into a catastrophe."

Never has Dole been more adamant, and more visible, in a foreign policy debate than in the case of Bosnia. For him, this is not a complicated matter. He gets to attack the Democratic president against whom he hopes to run on a matter of obvious importance to him.

And one on which he is convinced he is right.

Dole has regularly assailed President Clinton for his reluctance to take a strong position on Bosnia. In July of 1995, he said, "We've been waiting and waiting and waiting for leadership, and so far, nothing has happened."

To be sure, it's easier to be critical when you're *not* the fellow in the White House. But as Dole noted, he was merely treating Clinton as Clinton had treated Bush in 1992, when the Democratic challenger urged lifting the arms embargo so that Bosnian Muslims could get more sophisticated weaponry.

"It is indeed ironic that the Clinton Administration—whose policy in Bosnia needs to be checked hourly—is on attack against those in Congress like myself who have consistently argued for a policy that candidate Clinton advocated."

Late in 1995, when Clinton did take a firm position on Bosnia, sending U.S. troops to enforce a U.S.-brokered peace agreement, Dole supported him—reluctantly, grudgingly, but adequately.

Economic Policy

As a leading member of the Senate Finance Committee, Dole has been heavily involved in *fiscal* policy—taxes, the federal budget, the deficit. He hasn't played as big a role in *economic* policy, where his views tend to moderation.

Farm belt senators tend to view economic policy largely through the perspective of the grain farmer. That means they like easy credit, juicy export subsidies, and a dollar that isn't too strong. Dole has been no exception. In the summer of 1986, when farmers were grumbling, he offered this analysis: "If you're losing money because you can't export or have lost your farm because there's no market for your grain, the number one culprit is probably the high dollar, which has dropped recently 20 to 25 percent. The result is the trade deficit is now falling, and I've seen a more aggressive attitude toward free trade in the administration in the last six months. By the end of the year, Congress will probably pass legislation mandating the administration to take certain actions if we determine that there has been injury in this country because of unfair trade practices. This is not protectionism, however."

Like most farm state senators, he never met a grain embargo he liked. When President Carter blocked grain sales to the Soviet Union after its invasion of Afghanistan, Dole said, "Carter took a poke at the Soviet bear and knocked out the American farmer."

In the recession of 1991, Dole got caught in between the Democratic majorities in the Congress, who wanted to extend unemployment benefits, and the Republican president, who did not.

Like a good partisan soldier, Dole supported his president. Defending Bush's veto of the Democratic bill, Dole charged that Democrats were seeking "political benefits at the expense of unemployed Americans."

This was, by all indications, one of those occasions on which Dole was carrying water for the administration rather than following his core beliefs or instincts.

When the White House later dropped its opposition and Congress passed a Democratic bill that it knew Bush would sign, Dole's "aye" was the loudest on the floor, and he later explained his discomfort with his earlier position. "My view—'We don't want to give anybody unemployment benefits'—was not a winner."

SCANDALS

Until they get really bad, political scandals tend to get partisan reactions.

Accuse a Democrat, and the Democrats will become civil libertarians concerned with how the accused pol is innocent until proven guilty, while the Republicans will become moralistic prosecutors demanding full hearings, quickly followed by the gibbet, or at least the pillory.

Perhaps because he was once burned by Watergate, perhaps because his own public life has been all but untouched by a hint of impropriety, Dole is something of an exception to this rule.

And he did get burned by Watergate. The wisecracks he started to make about it a few years later tend to obscure the reality that as Republican national chairman he was part of the White House counterattack team in 1972. When Nixon's opponent, George McGovern, started suggesting that there might be some White House involvement in the break-in at Democratic headquarters, Dole punched back.

"For the last week, the Republican party has been the victim of a barrage of unfounded and unsubstantiated allegations by George McGovern and his partner-in-mudslinging, the *Washington Post*. Given the present straits in which the McGovern campaign finds itself, Mr. McGovern appears to have turned over the franchise for his media attack campaign to the editors of the *Washington Post,* who have shown themselves every bit as sure-footed along the low road of this campaign as their candidate."

A couple of weeks later, after a few more damaging stories in the *Post*, Dole was back on the warpath. In Baltimore, he told a meeting of the Maryland Republican State Central Committee, "The greatest political scandal of this campaign is the brazen manner in which, without benefit of clergy, the *Washington Post* has set up housekeeping with the McGovern campaign. With his campaign collapsing around his ears, Mr. McGovern some weeks back became the beneficiary of the most extensive journalistic rescue-and-salvage operation in American politics.

"The *Post*'s reputation for objectivity and credibility have sunk so low they have almost disappeared from the Big Board altogether.

"There is a cultural and social affinity between the McGovernites and the *Post* executives and editors. They belong to the same elite; they can be found living cheek-by-jowl in the same exclusive chic neighborhoods, and hobnobbing at the same Georgetown parties.

"There is the historic *Post* hostility to the person and political fortunes of the president of the United States—dating from the days of Alger Hiss when the president was proven right, and the *Post* and its friends exposed as gullible and naive.

"It is only the *Washington Post* which deliberately mixes together illegal and unethical episodes, like the Watergate Caper, with shenanigans which have been the stock-in-trade of political pranksters from the day I came into politics.

"Now Mr. Bradlee,[3] an old Kennedy coat-holder, is entitled to his views. But when he allows his paper to be used as a political instrument of the McGovernite campaign; when he himself travels the country as a small-bore McGovern surrogate—then he and his publication should expect appropriate treatment—which they will with regularity receive."

And in September, when a grand jury indicted three of the Watergate conspirators but no White House officials, Dole claimed that this proved the falseness of "any of the wild and slanderous statements McGovern has been making."

So when it turned out that McGovern's statements had been tame and accurate, as were the stories in the *Washington Post*, Dole was chastened.

---

[3]Ben Bradlee, then the *Washington Post* editor.

When the Iran-Contra scandal was at its peak, for instance, Dole could defend President Reagan. But he wasn't about to give everyone in the administration a pass. "He didn't make mistakes. The people around him made mistakes. I think right now they ought to circle the wagons—either that, or let a couple of wagons go over the cliff."

But just because he was defending Reagan, Dole saw no need to defend anyone else, no matter how close to Reagan they were. As to George Shultz, for instance, Dole noted, "I must say, when people say, 'Why aren't you out there supporting the president?', it's rather difficult when the secretary of state is not doing anything."

And just in case anyone thought Dole was getting subtle, he made a speech in which he pronounced the entire Iran-Contra operation "just plain stupid."

Dole is more apt to jump on Democrats than Republicans when they get into trouble. But sometimes he restrains himself altogether. He has said relatively little about the mini-scandal known as Whitewater. And in public at least, he has been cautious in defense of Oregon Republican Senator Bob Packwood, who was accused of sexual transgressions.

He did dismiss one of the earlier—and more dismissable—moves against Packwood. When some angry Oregonians claimed that Packwood's reelection should be invalidated because he had "defrauded" his state's voters, Dole's response was unequivocal: "Is every election in which the winning candidate made a false or misleading statement up for grabs?"

If it were, Dole knew, Packwood's would not be the only seat at risk.

Later, when California Democratic Senator Barbara Boxer unsuccessfully tried to force the Senate Ethics Committee to hold public hearings on the Packwood case, Dole had this sarcastic and scornful suggestion on revamping the entire system of policing Senate ethics: "Why don't we turn it over to the senator from California?"

Dole showed no restraint, though, in attacking the prolonged investigation and prosecution of the Iran-Contra scandal. In May of 1991, almost five years after the scandal first broke, Dole angrily called for abolishing the special counsel's office headed by Lawrence Walsh. "Spring has come and gone. There are no new indictments. It is now time for history, and not the courts, to be the final judge of the Iran-Contra affair. It's time that Mr. Walsh and his staff do the taxpayers a favor by closing their investigation and removing themselves from the government payroll."

Walsh persisted, and subsequently indicted former Defense Secretary Caspar Weinberger. When, on December 24, 1992, the lame duck Bush pardoned Weinberger and five other former government officials, Dole celebrated the proclamation as a "Christmas Eve act of courage and compassion. Lawrence Walsh and his desperate henchmen would have stopped at nothing to validate their reckless $35 million inquisition, even if it meant twisting justice to fit their partisan scheme."

So angry was Dole that he helped other Republicans block reauthorization of the special counsel law. That was in 1992.

A year later he had changed his mind. By then, there was a Democratic president, and Dole did not deny that this influenced his switch. "If there was ever a need, it is when one party controls everything."

Early in the Clinton Administration, when it turned out that administration officials had suggested using the Internal Revenue Service to investigate irregularities at the White House Travel Office if the FBI wouldn't cooperate, Dole joined (or perhaps began) the anti-government tone of the Republican opposition. "The most terrifying letters in the English language are FBI and IRS."

He was more tolerant of an intraparty foe, Phil Gramm. He may not think much of Gramm. He may be running against him for the nomination. But when Gramm was accused of wrongdoing, Dole acted as the commander taking care of one of his troops.

The allegation, which came from the "citizens lobby" Common Cause, was that Gramm had paid only part of the cost of completing his vacation home, and had then helped the contractor in some difficulties with federal regulators.

To Dole, it was anti-Republican nonsense. He called it, "The latest attempt to nail a Republican, even when there is absolutely no evidence to support its accusations. This is a closed matter. The Ethics Committee has already reviewed the facts and ruled that there was nothing improper."

Gramm had told the Ethics Committee about his price break, but not about helping the contractor with the regulators.

Now, as to Dole's own integrity, the only hint of scandal that ever touched Dole personally has to do with an apartment in Florida. It's in the Sea View Hotel, a cooperatively owned oceanfront resort in Bal Harbour, and the Doles are hardly the only celebrated owners.

On the contrary, the place has been a bipartisan Florida retreat. Howard Baker had a place there and so did former Democratic Chairman Robert Strauss and the late Speaker of the House, Tip O'Neill. The Doles bought their apartment (technically they bought seventy-five shares of the co-op) in 1982 for $150,000.

That was cheap. Three months earlier an almost-identical unit in a less desirable spot in the building was sold for $190,000. The *New York Times* later hired an accountant who said that the Doles' unit should have cost that much, too.

So? What's wrong with getting a good deal?

Maybe nothing. In this case, though, the good deal was arranged for the Doles by Dwayne Andreas, the chairman of Archer Daniels Midland (ADM), the multi-billion-dollar agricultural commodities company.

To say that ADM has an interest in legislation is to understate reality. It is, for instance, the leading American producer of ethanol, the market for which depends in part on federal subsidies. Dole supports those subsidies.

But then, so do almost all members of Congress from the farm states.

Dole points that out, and also says that the apartment technically is not his, but only his wife's. "It's not my property, so I don't run around keeping numbers on it. Check with Elizabeth. She bought it."

But in both of their names.

As to his support for ethanol subsidies, he said, "There is a lot of interest in ethanol; it didn't all come from ADM."

HOLLYWOOD

Shortly after he announced his candidacy for 1996, Dole went to Hollywood to complain about how it portrayed America to itself. "A line has been crossed—not just of taste, but of human dignity and decency. It is crossed every time sexual violence is given a catchy tune. When teen suicide is set to an appealing beat. When Hollywood's dream factories turn out nightmares of depravity."

Dole made it clear that he was not proposing censorship, nor was he objecting to movie companies making big bucks. But he assailed the "corporate executive who hides behind the lofty language of free speech in order to profit from the debasing of America."

And he singled out the Time Warner company, which owned a record company that produces records with lyrics extolling violence. "There is a difference between the description of evil through art and the marketing of evil through commerce."

Later, reporters asked Dole about the $21,000 he had received over the years from Time-Warner's political action committee. "I think it demonstrates that they didn't buy anything with Bob Dole."

As to the likely reaction to his speech: "I probably won't get an Oscar for it."

Later, he repeated his opposition to censorship: "I would hope that we would not let the government take one inch, make one effort that would indicate that we are headed toward government regulation, government involvement—censorship, if you will—and give industry a chance to clean up its own act."

But, he noted, "Shame is a powerful weapon."

Facts and Figures

NAME: Robert Joseph Dole.

DATE OF BIRTH: July 22, 1923, in Russell, Kansas.

EDUCATION: Graduate of Russell public schools; attended University of Kansas, Lawrence; Bachelor of Arts from Washburn Municipal University, Topeka, 1952; LL.B., Washburn, 1952.

MILITARY SERVICE: Enlisted United States Army, 1943. Tenth Mountain Division platoon leader in Italy; twice wounded; decorated for "heroic achievement; discharged as captain, 1948.

RELIGION: Methodist.

THE QUOTABLE BOB DOLE

PERSONAL: Married to the former Elizabeth Hanford. One daughter, Robin, from a previous marriage.

ORGANIZATIONS: Kiwanis, 4-H Fair Association, B.P.O.E., Masons, Isis Shrine, Chamber of Commerce, American Legion, Veterans of Foreign Wars, Disabled American Veterans, National Society of Autistic Children, Dole Foundation (founder and chairman of the board).

OFFICE: Senior Senator from Kansas, Majority Leader.

SENATE COMMITTEES: Agriculture, Nutrition, and Forestry; Finance; Rules and Administration.

1994 INTEREST GROUP RATINGS
(percentage of votes favorable to each organization)

Americans for Democratic Action	0
American Civil Liberties Union	26
COPE (AFL-CIO)	0
Consumer Federation of America	25
League of Conservation Voters	0
Concord Coalition	82
National Security Index	100
American Conservative Union	100
National Tax Limitation Committee	88
Christian Coalition	100

Notes on Sources

Nothing herein qualifies as what the historians would call a primary source. Every one of these quotes from Bob Dole has been quoted before by a writer, and in only one case (on page 97) was I that writer.

Because this is supposed to be a popular book, not a scholarly tome, I have not provided source footnotes, so the reader will not know where any individual quote first appeared. Be assured, though, that what follows is based on a prodigious amount of research, some of it by Karen Blair of Chicago, who can find any piece of information that anyone in the world has ever put on line.

As a low-tech kind of guy, I did the book part myself, examining the index of every responsible[4]

---

[4] OK, and a few not so responsible.

book written about public affairs in America in the last thirty years, or at least every one that could be found at the Harold Washington Library in Chicago or the Bailey-Howe Library, the University of Vermont's main library in Burlington. If Bob Dole's name was in that index (and it was in far too many), his words and actions got checked out.

In only a few cases, have I deemed it necessary to mention the source. A couple of quotes, for instance, are from Jeb Magruder's book, and though Mr. Magruder has paid his debt to society, I thought the reader was entitled to know when an account came from someone whose veracity has been questioned in official legal proceedings.

One or two of the quotes seem to have been evoked by the interviewing techniques of the writer. In those cases, I have given them credit.

Most of the Dole words repeated here were spoken in public—in speeches, at press conferences, or in interviews on radio and television. I heard a few of them over the air and got more from transcripts. But most came from newspapers or magazines. The largest number are from the *New York Times.* Others are from the *Chicago Tribune,* the *Washington Post,* the *Boston Globe, Time,* and the *New York Times Magazine.*

Most of the words of Bob Dole that are quoted here but which were *not* uttered in a public forum come from books, mostly books written about the presidential campaigns of 1980 and 1988, and the accounts of the Reagan and Bush presidencies, in which Dole played an important part as the Republican leader in the Senate.

In some cases, these writers themselves did not hear Dole's words, but relied on accounts from the campaign aides or government officials who had worked with (or, sometimes, against) the senator. Every one of the writers who reported these quotes is a respected journalist or a high-ranking government official of the Reagan or Bush administrations.

Most of the more private, intimate quotations from Bob Dole come either from *What It Takes*, Richard Ben Cramer's superb book about the 1988 election, or from *Bob Dole, American Political Phoenix*, the critical but admiring biography by Stanley G. Hilton, once a senior member of Dole's Senate staff.

A complete list of the books consulted for information for this book follows.

Jack Germond and Jules Witcover, *Blue Smoke and Mirrors*, Viking Press, 1981.

Jack Germond and Jules Witcover, *Whose Broad Stripes and Bright Stars?*, Warner Books, 1989.

Richard Ben Cramer, *What It Takes*, Random House, 1992.

Stanley G. Hilton, *Bob Dole: America's Political Phoenix*, Contemporary Books, 1988.

Jules Witcover, *Crapshoot: Rolling the Dice on the Vice Presidency*, Crown Books, 1992.

Sidney Blumenthal, *The Rise of the Counter-establishment*, Times Books, 1986.

George Schultz, *Toil and Turmoil*, Scribners, 1993.

Bruce Oudes, editor, *From: The President. Richard Nixon's Secret Files*, Harper & Row, 1989.

Myra MacPherson, *The Power Lovers*, G.P. Putnam's Sons, 1975.

J. Lee Annis, Jr., *Howard Baker: Conciliator in an Age of Crisis*, Madison Books, 1995.

H.R. Haldeman, *The Haldeman Diaries*, Putnam, 1994.

J. Anthony Lukas, *Nightmare: the Underside of the Nixon Years*, Viking Press, 1973.

Bob Woodward and Carl Bernstein, *The Final Days*, Simon & Schuster, 1976.

Elizabeth Drew, *American Journal*, Random House, 1976.

Hamilton Jordan, *Crisis: the Last Year of the Carter Presidency*, G.P. Putnam's Sons, 1982.

Donald Regan, *For the Record*, Harcourt, 1988.

Sidney Blumenthal, *Pledging Allegiance*, HarperCollins, 1990.

Lou Cannon, *President Reagan: The Role of a Lifetime*, Simon & Schuster, 1991.

Peter Goldman and Tom Mathews, *The Quest for the Presidency, 1988*, Touchstone, 1989.

Bob Dole and Elizabeth Dole with Richard Norton Smith, *Unlimited Partners*, Simon & Schuster, 1988.